CHRISTIANITY UNLEASHED

SLAVES TO SOLDIERS

MARC CARRIER

www.ChristianityUnleashed.net

Contents

Acknowledgements

First and foremost I want to thank our Heavenly Father; my Lord and King, Jesus Christ; and the Teacher and Comforter, the Holy Spirit for being very patient with me and taking me on this journey and adventure. It is my privilege to serve our God, and I pray this book will be pleasing to Him. I also want to thank my wonderful wife and helper, Cindy, who has not only patiently endured my personal growth these years, but also has proven an exceptional editor, writer, and sounding board during the publishing process. I am grateful for brothers Jonathan Ammon, Chris Burton, Glenn Roseberry, and Reed Merino for taking their time to read the manuscript and provide valuable edits and comments. I also want to thank my son, Isaiah, who lent great insight during project development and prepared an excellent cover. Lastly, I appreciate all my brothers and sisters, African and American, who have walked this story out with me. I could not have done the ministry without you, let alone have a story to tell. God bless all of you.

Introduction

I have served on the mission field in Kenya and Uganda with my family since 2012. Struggles and mistakes, punctuated by periods of encouragement, marked the early years of my ministry here. We focused on kingdom expansion, strong discipleship, and the development of indigenous leaders, and continually pressed forward in meeting these goals. Yet no matter how much progress we made, there so often seemed to be *something missing*. I was given a clue, but not total clarity, when I wrote a book about my field experiences (*Pioneering the Kingdom*), and sent it to a Facebook friend for review. His comment, essentially, was that the book had a lot going for it, but he quite pointedly asked, "Where is the Holy Spirit?"

Indeed, though I had begun my work in Africa with a sense of calling and a leading of the Holy Spirit, I somehow lost it. The goal of this book is to share how that happened, and how the Holy Spirit was restored, as I believe that in our Christian walk we are all at risk of beginning in the Spirit but falling away for various reasons. This is my testimony and I will share many stories, some from my early Christian experience in America and others from the mission field. In it, you will see that walking in the power and leading of the Holy Spirit is God's desire for every believer, not just those "called" to ministry or missions.

Throughout the book, you will find endnotes referring to quotes from the "Ante-Nicene" church, the time period encompassing the first few hundred years after Christ's death and resurrection. Why are these significant? Imagine a stream flowing from a clear mountain source; over time and distance, it gradually picks up debris and by the time it reaches the mouth where it empties, it is muddied—a far cry from the purity of its beginnings. The same is true of church history; the farther we get from its humble yet powerful beginnings, the more uncertainty and disagreement we experience. The Ante-Nicene period is significant because these men were the disciples of the apostles of Christ or not far removed. They understood the Scriptures at a level that we (despite our modern scholarship) likely do not, as it described their contemporary culture and was written in their language. They had a purity of Christian experience (culminating in martyrdom for many, if not most), that over time has been lost. Therefore, as you read, I urge you to refer to the quotes, as they substantiate many of the points I make and certainly concur with my field experience and the straightforward reading of the Scriptures.

This book does not just describe my journey, but invites you to experience the same transformation: to walk in the power and leading of the Holy Spirit in the way that God has meant for us all from the very beginning, but which we have, in some sense, lost along the way. This journey is not for the faint-hearted. As you will see, it demands the courage and conviction of a warrior and the perseverance of a dedicated soldier. Join me!

Chapter 1—From Slaves to Soldiers

A proud king with a great army demands the submission of a neighboring king, whose forces are small but courageous. When an ambassador delivers the message requesting complete surrender, the king with the smaller army at once summons one of his men and commands that the soldier stab himself. Without hesitation, he complies. This is repeated with a second soldier, and yet a third. Satisfied, the king gives his response to the ambassador's demand: "Go and tell your master that I have three thousand such men; let him come."

This story from antiquity, shared in Andrew Murray's classic, *A Life of Obedience*, shows us the disposition of the type of soldier that God calls to the front lines of battle against the spiritual forces of evil. This was the spirit of the early Christians, who were willing to surrender themselves, even unto death, on behalf of their conquering King.

We imagine the apostles as just a ragtag band of twelve poor, uneducated men. They had little money, no political or institutional backing, no printed literature, and were facing extreme persecution—leading to martyrdom for most. Yet the Bible tells us that they turned the whole world upside down. Today's Christian is a descendent of this courageous group of men, yet we lack the same sense of urgency with which they pressed forward for the kingdom of God. How is it that with everything against them, they were able to succeed where we are failing?

Most Americans self-identify as Christian, but their practices tend to belie this assertion. Even more telling is that, when surveyed whether they thought that they had a personal responsibility for evangelism, a majority does not believe that they do.[i]

Just as in the time of the apostles, there is a battle waging between God and Satan. Yet as the battle cry goes out today, it remains largely unanswered. Today's Christian is called to engage in the battle, yet due to the subversive tactics of our enemy, many aren't even aware that we are at war. We are losing our own to the world. Research demonstrates that most of our youth are unchurched,[ii] while the majority who grow up in the church fall away anyway.[ii] It is clear that our institutions, programs, and doctrines have proven powerless to stop the attrition.

The human spirit yearns for the purpose, adventure, and fulfillment evident in the life of the early church—men who abandoned all to follow Christ. Having nothing, they possessed everything. Hear their own testimony of a life of sacrifice and adventure:

> Even as things are, if your thought is to spend this period of existence in enjoyments, how are you so ungrateful as to consider insufficient, as not thankfully to recognize the many and exquisite pleasures God has bestowed upon you? For what is more delightful than to have God the Father and our Lord at peace with us, than revelation of the truth, than confession of our errors, than pardon of the innumerable sins of our past life? What greater pleasure than distaste of pleasure itself, contempt of all that the world offers, true liberty, a pure conscience, a contented life, and freedom from all fear of death? What is nobler than to tread underfoot the gods of the nations—to expel evil spirits—to perform healings—to seek divine revelations—to live to God? These are the pleasures, these are the entertainments worthy of Christian men—holy, everlasting, free. Consider these as your circus games, fix your eyes on the courses of the world, the changing seasons, reckon up the periods of time, long for the goal of the final consummation, defend the assemblies of the churches, be startled at God's signal, be roused up at the angel's trumpet, glory in the hands of martyrdom. (Tertullian, *ANF* v. 3, 91. c. 197 AD)

We can regain what has been lost if we simply return to what we read about in the New Testament: spectacular conversions, amazing healings, demons fleeing at the dreaded name of Jesus, and awesome miracles testifying to the reality of a risen Lord. If we embrace this call, we will find the true joy of serving Christ, who is worthy of every sacrifice. Such service goes beyond the call of duty and reflects a desire to give our all for the Lord who has given us His all.

There is a war raging: God versus Satan, the kingdom of God diametrically opposed to the kingdom of darkness whose shadow falls across the entire world. Satan has amassed an army for the final battle against God, and it is time for us to join in the fight against him. Thus far, he has the fallen angels and all the demons on his side.[iii] His goal is, and always has been, to increase his force by turning as many humans as possible against their Creator.

All the way back to the Fall, man's predisposition to sin manifested itself. The result for Adam and Eve, and for all of us, was rebellion against God and bondage to Satan and sin (Romans 6:16). Though man was originally given dominion of the world (Genesis 1:26-28), God's arch-enemy deceived him. In a move that man could never have foreseen, Satan thus became the *de facto* ruler of this world and we became his slaves (Luke 4:6).

Of course, God was not oblivious to Satan's plans. He sent His Son, Jesus, to deliver us from our enslavement to Satan, sin, and the world, and to transfer us into His kingdom instead (Colossians 1:13-

14). What our modern gospel may fail to communicate is that our freedom from captivity was not meant to simply spare us from our deserved punishment. No—it was meant to free us from Satan's power and compel us to fight against the enemy. We are not just citizens of a new kingdom, but enlisted soldiers. Once saved, we are intended to engage against all the powers of darkness. Instead, our shrewd foe has simply changed his tactics and successfully lulled us into complacency, so that most are completely unaware of his methods and plans.

Satan's work is two-fold. First, knowing that by default man is on his side, he wants to keep him from defecting and finding freedom (through salvation). Failing this, our enemy works all the more feverishly to prevent man from gathering more of Satan's own troops against him to undermine his chances for victory. Just one soul changing allegiance from the kingdom of darkness to the kingdom of light, and actively engaging in gathering more souls through ongoing discipleship, is an undeniable threat to Satan.

Once "saved," most Christians accept their perceived freedom, but many are oblivious to Satan's persistence in his effort to render them entirely ineffective and unproductive for the advancement of God's kingdom. Through an impressive variety of means (some defined by Jesus in Matthew 13:20-22 as affliction, persecution, worry, and the deceitfulness of wealth), the enemy succeeds in keeping these unproductive believers on a tight leash, where they are ultimately unable to fight their way to the front lines of the battle. Instead of seeking to bring the message of freedom to the lost around them, they are distracted by the worries and cares of the world.

Jesus said the harvest is ready, but the laborers are few (Luke 10:2). Where are they? Multitudes are deceived by the wiles of the enemy, very often strongholds that are developed right within their own religious factions. Unlike the early Christians who accepted the call to count the cost and surrender everything for their Lord, today our ranks are filled with people who think it's enough to attend regular meetings and live a "good" life. They are seldom told there is a war going on, let alone trained and sent to fight in it.

Just as Satan has a two-fold plan of attack, the purposes of *Christianity Unleashed* are also two-fold. The first goal is to expose the enemy's program and *unleash* those who are bound in slavery to Satan; the second goal is to train, mobilize, and *unleash* a flood of front-line soldiers for the battle to plunder the kingdom of darkness. Every saint can be prepared and equipped to engage in the battle in the same way, with the same spirit, and with the same tools as the early Christians. God wants soldiers who are willing to give all in their service to Him—not just out of duty, but with sincere devotion and love for Him.

The battle against the kingdom of darkness is, of course, a spiritual battle fought with spiritual weapons (Ephesians 6:10-18). Yet the determination, sacrifice, and honor of a hero are still demanded of those who engage in front-line warfare. Far from being a life of duty and drudgery, we experience vibrant purpose, exciting adventure, and deep fulfillment as we step forward into the abundant Christian life that we see in the book of Acts. Join me in becoming a front-line soldier for the kingdom of God, walking not in wise and persuasive words, but in demonstrations of the Holy Spirit and of power (1 Corinthians 2:4). In the next chapter, I'll share how that transition happened for me, in hopes that you also will look more deeply at what God has done, and can do, in your own life.

Chapter 2—The Enemy Strikes and the Holy Spirit Retaliates

A man was escorting me through a terminal of sorts, like a train or airport terminal. The enormous cavern of a facility was of light gray, stone construction. It was well-lit, yet lacked any windows or any view outside the building—as if it were closed in or it was just dark outside. The terminal was very long and bustling with activity; in the background I could hear what I presumed were announcements of arrivals and departures. Curiously, I did not see any of the normal carts or baggage that one commonly finds accompanying travelers, though numerous people were there.

My escort suddenly remarked, "What are you doing here? You are not permitted to be here."

I responded, "You tell me. You're the one escorting me."

He continued on as if I hadn't spoken, and as we walked I began to notice others in the terminal. Several were loitering around, sitting on or leaning on benches or rails. Others were going to and fro, oblivious to anything but their own agenda. But remarkably, they were all men—no women or children. One in particular caught my attention. He was extremely handsome, with dirty blond hair and several days' growth of darker scruff on his face. I pegged him at about thirty-five or forty years-old, with an athletic build at just a tad over six feet tall. His clothes were business casual, what one would expect in a terminal such as this. Abruptly, he approached where I was standing.

My escort immediately appeared nervous and gave us some room. Then eerily, it became obvious that our handsome visitor could not see me at all, but he clearly sensed my unwelcome presence. He circled me, just inches away, and I both felt and heard an electrical discharge all around me as he moved. Suddenly, all the others in the terminal stood at attention, trying to discern why this man of importance was so interested in my location. Then, to my shock, his hazel eyes turned jet black. Immediately, several of the others present in the terminal likewise looked my way with jet black eyes. Alarmed, I realized that this was not an earthly terminal but rather a place in the heavenlies.

This explained the initial alarm of my escort, an angel himself, upon seeing me present there. And it became obvious that the other beings in my presence were angels—some good, and some evil. The biggest shock? I discerned the identity of the one who had taken a keen and sudden interest in me as Satan himself!

As quickly as I had become the center of attention, Satan apparently finished his reconnaissance and noted nothing of concern.

He nonchalantly walked away from whence he came. The others returned to their loitering or activities. *Phew*! Close call, indeed.

My escort again joined me and brought me to the entrance of a room full of men donned in suits and ties wearing dark glasses—classic FBI-looking folks. They were discussing the imminent landfall of a serious natural disaster. I caught just that much before my escort urged me on.

We entered another room, and I was motioned to sit down. I was seated at a nondescript, light-colored, L-shaped table or bench with my angel friend on the other side. He had in his hand a book, what appeared to be a little diary of sorts. He tried to hand it to me. As he extended his hand to me, I noted a second book right in front of me. I asked him what was in that one. He slid it away from me a bit and told me to never mind that book. But that only piqued my curiosity. *What could be in that forbidden little book*? I wondered to myself. I persevered in my desire to see it, but he continued to refuse me permission and advised me repeatedly to disregard it. Stubbornly, I refused to relent and finally, took the book into my hands and opened it.

Each page contained a brief log—primarily a date and a description, while some pages had official-looking notes or stamps. I read the first page—*whoa*! These were logs of personal sins that I had committed in my youth—things I scarcely remembered, but upon review, I could confirm the accuracy of the accounts.

As I perused the small book, the seriousness of the content caused internal pangs of conviction and sadness such that I found myself sobbing as I read the logs. As I continued to weep uncontrollably, the angel withdrew the offer of the second book that he had intended to give me. I awoke with a lingering sense of fear and regret. I don't want to presume any theological significance, but upon waking I did note that the log only contained records up to the time that I gave my life to Christ. Perhaps this was why I was repeatedly advised by the angel to disregard it. It was the night of August 25, 2005.

Four days later, Hurricane Katrina hit Southeast Louisiana, killing over 1,200 people and resulting in over $100 billion in damage. Memory of the natural disaster referenced in the angels' discussion in the dream was still fresh in my mind, and the rest would take on much greater significance as time went on.

Fast-forward to late 2016. After five years in East Africa, we could count hundreds of disciples and dozens of churches in three countries. I was now splitting my time between the mature mission in Western Kenya and a fledgling mission in Eastern Uganda. I was returning from the Uganda mission to the Kenya mission around the holidays and found real challenges—spiritual warfare at a whole new level. We had experienced spiritual warfare before, to be certain, but things seemed to have escalated this time.

Three of our disciples had just been in serious accidents, though all were miraculously preserved from injury. We buried two children of the brethren. One of our workers was being threatened with bodily harm because of his association with me. And, it seemed that the unity and enthusiasm of the Kenya mission was at an all-time low. I put out an urgent call to prayer on Facebook and started fasting and praying as 2017 began.

Over quite some time, beginning as early as 2009 and right through 2017, the Lord had given me forebodings of my untimely death. There was not really a one-time revelation that I could point to, but rather a combination of dreams, visions, and interpretations all lending themselves to this conclusion.

It was not as if I walked in fear each day, expecting an assault or traffic accident. I felt comfortable leaving it in the Lord's hands, but I operated on the keen understanding that there would be big change in the life of my family and in the future of the mission as the events I anticipated unfolded.

Though this may seem extreme, maybe even far-fetched, I had confidence in what I was hearing from God. I found that as I grew spiritually over my years as a Christian, God was faithful to increasingly reveal things of import to me (often through dreams) so that I could act upon the information. Needless to say, I had come to trust in warnings and words from the Lord.

Thus, as spiritual warfare erupted over the Kenya mission, forebodings of my potentially impending death were not far from my mind. I recalled one particularly confusing dream, as suddenly it seemed relevant to the current events.

In the dream, strife was rampant on the mission and my family was in the middle of it all, prey to the cultural strongholds that were at the root of the battle. I was traveling on foot with a band of brothers, seeking refuge from the ongoing struggles. Though I desperately wanted to find a better place and was convinced that that was where I was headed, I was torn. I had only to look back and see the ongoing strife and confusion—my family amidst the chaos. I wondered, *do I keep walking forward, or do I go back*? One of the companions in my group told me I was the only one with the power to bring peace to the turmoil left behind. I paused, conflicted, as the others walked determinedly on. Eventually, I was left alone. But the Lord assured me, even in my sleep, that He had not left me. I awoke with a start.

As I meditated on then-current events and this dream recalled from the past, I could see that I would come to a point of decision. During the time of strife, I could remain behind and continue ministering, also bringing stability to my family, or I would be permitted to move on to a better place—which to me, seemed obviously to relate to the premonitions of my death. In the dream, as in reality, I was torn. For as the apostle Paul said, *to live is Christ, and to die is gain.* Yet even he knew that he would remain for the sake of the brethren (see Philippians 1:21-26).

I became even more convinced of these conclusions when my wife, Cindy, received a confirming message from the Lord that spoke to her personally about my death. I'm not one to hide things from my family; they were aware of everything I felt the Lord had revealed to me, so this was no surprise. Cindy and I agreed that in the event of my death, the family was to move back to America.

Even my son, Jonah, felt that he was hearing from the Lord about events that were to unfold. He has always been an animal lover and usually had a special pet—typically, a cat. His current feline was an orange and white female named Buttercup, who always came to curl up on Jonah's lap during family devotions. Jonah's attachment to "Bussy," as she was nicknamed, made him concerned for what would happen to her if the worst happened and the family moved back stateside. Though he did not ask the Lord for a sign, he did pray that God would have Bussy "disappear" before such an event, so that she would not think that Jonah had abandoned her. While we were in Uganda, sometime late in 2016, Bussy did indeed disappear from our Kenya home. The significance of it was not lost on any of us when we returned to Kenya, and she was simply not to be found.

Yet surprisingly, we were all at peace with these various developments and simply prayed that the Lord's will be done. All we could do was put one foot in front of the other as each day and its events unfolded. Jesus was right when He said that we shouldn't be anxious about tomorrow, because today has enough worries of its own (Matthew 6:34).

Our primary concern was the mission in spiritual disarray, which centered on a few of our local home fellowships. Interestingly, one of the satellite fellowships, not involved in these difficulties, had recently started all-night prayer meetings, which were now beginning to take hold and bear fruit. The brethren there were seeing God move in powerful new ways: demons cast out, miraculous healings, and prophetic words.

These powerful prayer meetings, my Facebook friends praying, and my personal prayer and fasting all converged during this point of crisis early in 2017. I did not know when I would finish my fast, but determined to persevere until the Lord intervened. I prayed in earnest that the Lord would work a miracle in the mission. The answer to all these supplications was a surprise indeed.

As it turned out, the Lord had a mighty work to do in *me* before He could do a work in the mission itself. Isolated and seeking God intently, He reminded me of an ongoing struggle that I yearned to be free from, but which always seemed to keep me in bonds. I was exposed to pornography beginning at age five; by my teen-age years, and even into my early marriage, I considered it a normal part of life. When my wife and I became Christians, that view radically changed and I abandoned porn without a backward glance. What troubled me, however, was that so many of the images I saw from my impressionable youth were burned into my mind. They were conjured up against my every will and desire, at a moment's notice. As much as I earnestly desired my mind to be washed of these images, I simply could not escape their grasp. There was nothing I could do to get free.

A second revelation concerned the hardening of my heart after arriving in Africa. I began with great spiritual fervor and the feeling of a true calling, but Africa was hard on all of us—especially me. Even before I got off the plane, my Kenyan bank account was emptied of the money which I had set aside for a car. Books for which I had previously sent funds were not printed. My work permit was not approved as promised, and now the people who had invited us here were working hard to try to kick us out of the country and even threatening harm to my family. Once the Lord delivered us from those trials, the next round of offenses ensued. Over time, I did grow a bit wiser and more attentive to the Lord's guidance, but the cycle of betrayals and troubles bore its bad fruit in the form of a hardened heart, which made my ongoing ministry a challenge. I knew I needed the Lord to intervene and help me. One thing I saw was that I needed to stop viewing people as the problem, but rather recognize the true enemy, Satan. He wanted to paralyze the mission and stop God's work, and unfortunately, I had become an unwitting co-conspirator in his plan.

As far back as 2004, our family had abandoned all secular movies and entertainment, along with many other pursuits which we felt competed with our interest in the Lord's work. Yet American missionaries, of all people, would visit Kenya and leave us with pirated films—some Christian, and some not—and we made excuses for watching them. Truthfully, they were a handy distraction from the realities of a mission that was more flesh than Spirit at that point. With some sense of conviction, over time we eventually stopped watching all but "Christian" films—with one notable exception, *Star Wars*. That was about to change.

When I was fasting, the Lord gave me a profound revelation: that Darth Vader was a real, *I mean very real*, demon. No way! It's just fantasy fiction, right? Well, I was convicted that Darth Vader was no less fictitious than Zeus or Hermes. Don't forget that when Paul talked about various "idols" of his day, he acknowledged that real demons did, in fact, work through those objects (1 Corinthians 10:20). That came as a serious shock to me. I felt that I had inadvertently permitted, and even invited, demonic activity into my home, and that it was time for some serious house cleaning.

Pornographic memories, Kenyan mission issues, and demonic activity manifested through media were issues brought to the forefront early on in my fast. I knew that unwanted spirits and their strongholds were at the root of all three. I had experience dealing with spiritual strongholds, which are loosely defined as lies of the enemy that we come to believe, and I knew that they could simply be overcome through the prayer of faith. (We'll return to this subject in greater detail in Chapter 8.) Whereas early in my Christian walk I had viewed pornography as a sin requiring repentance (which I had done), I now saw its ongoing work in my life as a stronghold that could be renounced. I rebuked the spirit of pornography and associated lust verbally, and felt immediately freed. In fact, since that time I have found that I can't conjure up any images from my past pornographic exposure.

Likewise, I identified a very distinct lack of love and spirit of bitterness in regard to the Kenya mission. Confessing it as Satan's work and not the fault of individuals, I renounced all his efforts in this area, and found my heart totally changed. Acknowledging the corrupting influence of media as well (and the underlying spirits), we purged our home—phones, computers, and bookshelves—of anything in the least bit suspect. Shockingly, the entire family completely agreed with this course of action, and we burned a great heap of stuff that day.

The work in me through fasting and prayer was just the beginning of what God would do. As I continued my fast, I repented more deeply for my failures with the Kenyan mission—specifically, for my inexcusable neglect of the leading and power of the Holy Spirit. As I considered how to remedy this deficiency, God brought to my recollection a local pastor named John. He had been a student of mine at a semester-long course on kingdom discipleship at a local Bible College. He had very authoritatively and assertively declared that the baptism of the Holy Spirit was the single most important aspect of discipleship. At the time, I did not argue the truth of his statement; however, I could not help but note that this was not the practice of our mission. He remarked that imparting the baptism of the Holy Spirit was one of his specialties—a gift. I received what he was saying because he was a very genuine man and I could sense his humble spirit, but at the time I simply filed our conversation away in my mental database.

As I recalled this discussion later, I knew we needed to invite the Holy Spirit into the Kenyan mission. However, I wasn't ready to go in alone and I figured it would be more like baby steps than a giant leap.

I immediately set out to find pastor John. I had to call a few contacts to get his number, but when we finally connected he was more than happy to come and meet with me. In fact, he was humbled and honored that his former instructor would remember him and seek his help.

I was excited but slightly apprehensive, not sure what I expected to happen as John, Titus and his wife, Christine, and I gathered together on that sunny Tuesday afternoon. But I was sure that something would. I had been doing front-line ministry for over a decade and yet up to that time, I had never initiated a disciple being baptized in the Holy Spirit. A couple of women had been filled with the Holy Spirit and even spoke in tongues during water baptism; however, God did it all, and I really had no intentionality or expectation of it. This day was different. This was intentional. When I considered what the Bible said on the subject, I recognized my weakness in this area and, quite honestly, was a bit insecure. Although I felt woefully inadequate for the job, I was certain of God's faithfulness. I knew I simply had to humble myself and allow Him to take the lead.

Pastor John began by teaching the biblical case for the baptism of the Holy Spirit. There were no verses or teachings new to me, nothing I was not already intimately familiar with. However, it was great for our disciples, Titus and Christine, to hear it from someone other than me. Afterwards, we all joined together in singing a few songs of worship.

Ni wewe,
Ni wewe Bwana,
Ni wewe!

The Spirit was clearly already at work as we lifted our voices in song and followed with prayer. In just a short time, Titus and Christine were overpowered by the Holy Spirit and fell on their faces, sobbing and repenting. John and I continued praying as the Holy Spirit obviously took them through some necessary healing. Then, quite effortlessly, Christine began speaking, and then praying, in tongues. John and I moved our attention to Titus. In just another minute, Titus was also overwhelmed by the Spirit and began speaking in tongues—not English, not Swahili, not Bukusu, but rather something completely unintelligible to all of us in the room.

When the din and excitement subsided, we praised God together. I was elated—all the teachings and examples presented in the Scriptures had manifested right here in my compound, with disciples that I had baptized.

The reality of the Holy Spirit was not new to me, yet as we had begun the transition from America to Kenya, we were involved with a self-described "kingdom" movement whose teachings functionally ignored the Holy Spirit. Though once I had received the baptism of the Holy Spirit myself and had been seeking His leading and work in my life, that aspect of my faith was gradually displaced by an emphasis on doctrinal agreement that originated with my kingdom brethren.

As I continued to fast and seek the Lord regarding all these things, a dear brother came to me privately and told me about a dream he had had two nights prior. He saw a multitude of people on a mountain looking downward at me in admiration. Then I picked up a book I had dropped some time earlier. I looked at the book and then moved to hand it over to one of my two boys, who were standing by me. Somewhat surprisingly, I skipped over Isaiah, my oldest son, who eagerly anticipated receiving it, and handed it to Enoch, my youngest. Isaiah immediately grew sullen. The onlookers on the mountain cheered.

I instantly knew the meaning. The mountain was the kingdom of God and the onlookers, the cloud of witnesses. My oldest son represented the capable, the talented, the knowledgeable, and experienced. Enoch, my youngest boy, represented the meek, the innocent—the pure heart of humility. The book was the one that I had been offered, yet ignored, in my dream of 2005, and it contained the things He was reminding me of afresh—walking in His power and leading. God had never taken the book from me; I had simply neglected it. And now I was to give it not to the learned, the capable in human terms. I was to hand it to the simple, the pure-hearted, the humble, and God would do His wonders. The book He gave me, I am now giving to *you*.

On the same day that my brother shared his dream with me, we had a *wazee* (elders) meeting. I taught specifically on receiving the baptism of the Holy Spirit and walking in His power and leading. I shared a little of my personal testimony as to what my Christian walk once was and how I had wandered away from the centrality of the Holy Spirit. I also told them that I had repented of my neglect. One brother stood up after the teaching and said very authoritatively, "The Marc we knew has died! He is now a new man."

His words resonated with me at a deep spiritual level. Had I been given new life through my repentance? During our family devotion time, I shared the report with my wife and children. I felt that clearly the Lord was telling me that the premonitions of my death were spiritual in nature, and that now God had given me a fresh start. I felt freed from any thought of my death. The family was a bit uncertain in this interpretation, but everyone seemed cautiously optimistic after having expected the worst for some time.

Cindy got up early the next morning to pray alone in the dark, as was her routine. She asked God if the *Mzee*'s (*mzee* means "older man" in Swahili) words really meant that I would not physically die. She would believe anything of the Lord, but there remained one point of confusion: what about Jonah's cat? We had been convinced that her disappearance had been a confirmation of what was to happen. Not many moments later, she heard a distinct *MEOW* pierce through the darkness. After an absence of more than a month, Jonah's cat had come home!

Though it was still much too early, Cindy excitedly ran to wake Jonah to tell him his beloved Bussy had returned. Suddenly, everyone was wiping the sleep from their eyes and we all took in the news, praising God for what He had been doing and for His encouragement.

The culmination of all these experiences reactivated my faith in earnest. We began to connect with the brethren in our network of churches, teaching and encouraging them to believe in and seek the baptism in the Holy Spirit. I invited pastor John to participate in two more of these meetings, then we were empowered to go in alone and do the same work ourselves.

Believing not only that the baptism and gifts of the Spirit were for today, but also believing that healings were still possible (see Mark 16:17-18), I started praying for people to be healed and WOW, I began to see things happen! Soon several of the disciples, men and women alike, were baptizing people in the Holy Spirit, healing people, and expelling demons. There was a palpable excitement when we gathered together and heard the testimonies of what God was doing. These were not far out people and places; these were brethren—our neighbors and friends. This was the new life I had neglected for oh-so-many years. Yet not only I, but an increasing number of my beloved brethren, were being equipped and mobilized for battle as front-line soldiers. We were experiencing the abundant life Jesus had promised, which just a short time ago had seemed like no more than words on a page. And although I did not yet know it, this was just the beginning of our living out the book of Acts today, serving in the battle for the kingdom. This is the life to which God calls us, and that He will make real to us, if we simply seek Him. It is my hope that the rest of this book will give you a battle plan and some weapons in your arsenal so that you can experience it more deeply for yourself.

Chapter 3—Personal Empowerment: Armed for Battle

In a marathon trip, my son, Isaiah, and I, along with a few of the Kenyan brethren (Luke, Titus and Christine, and their young son, Larry), made the trek to Uganda with the goal of introducing the baptism of the Holy Spirit to the Ugandan disciples. The sunny Sunday afternoon found us all praying fervently, with great anticipation of what God would do. We had already experienced much during the short visit, and it would be our last time together before returning to Kenya.

We sang and then prayed, feeling the heavy presence of the Holy Spirit as we gathered. I looked upward and could actually envision Jesus at the right hand of the Father. Prayerfully and reverently, I urged the Father to send the promised gift, the Holy Spirit, upon three of the Ugandan brethren who had gathered with us, expecting to experience God more deeply.

Suddenly, I waved my uplifted arms downward, as if to motion to the Holy Spirit to come down. Immediately, the brother on my left was baptized in the Holy Spirit and spoke in tongues. I repeated the arm motion as I continued to pray, petitioning the Father for the middle brother, and he fell to the ground in tears of repentance. I motioned and prayed again, for the brother to my right. He grew limp and then fell down, and we commanded an unclean spirit from him. When the brother was freed, we prayed that the Holy Spirit would come upon the repenting brother and he was filled. (The delivered brother was filled with the Holy Spirit at a future all-night prayer meeting).

It was the most amazing movement of God that I had experienced up to that point in my ministry. And I am certain that I would not have believed it if I had not participated in it myself. In the past, I had had my own questions about charismatic ministries and movements, but my invitation for the Holy Spirit to come was made in all sincerity, and He had simply responded to our heartfelt desire. We all praised God in amazement for what He had just done. Could our God really be so awesome and attentive to the cries of His saints? No words can adequately describe our feelings at that moment.

I don't consider myself particularly gifted or special. I wholeheartedly believe that everything God is doing in and through me is completely the work of the Holy Spirit and can be done by faith by any born-again Christian. Yet there is much confusion and division in the Christian community about even the things that I've shared thus far. It is therefore important that we understand the biblical basis for the ongoing work of the Holy Spirit, which is available to every

Christian. Unless you have knowledge, it is difficult to believe—and it is in believing that you will receive (Mark 11:24).

As you can see in my own testimony, one of the first things that I had to repent of in my ministry was the neglect of the baptism of the Holy Spirit, since it is just the beginning of greater things. Having developed a solid foundation of doctrine on repentance, baptism, and holiness with our Kenyan disciples, I expected a sudden emphasis on the work of the Holy Spirit to be a bit confusing for them. However, we needed to set things right in our mission, and I have a tendency to get things done faster rather than slower. I immediately began teaching both small groups and individuals that this promise of the Father was real, that it was freely available, and that they could receive it by faith. Every believer needs to have this understanding if they are going to experience the fullness of the Holy Spirit.

I would guess that most of us assume that Jesus' power (evidenced in the gospel accounts of His healings, casting out of demons, and miracles) was simply the result of His divinity—a trait that of course, no human being shares. Yet Philippians 2:5-8 reveals that Jesus voluntarily emptied Himself when He took on the form of a man. So where did His power come from?

Though the Scriptures say little about Jesus' early life, we know that He was just a small-town man who lived quietly as a carpenter. It is significant that even for Jesus, an encounter with the Holy Spirit was a precursor to His public ministry (see Luke 3:21-22). The presence of the fullness and leading of the Spirit in the life of Christ are further emphasized in Luke 4:1, 4:14, and 4:18. We see that with this in place, Jesus went out to teach with authority and with demonstrations of power. I don't believe this was a coincidence.

When Peter spoke to the Gentiles in Caesarea, he described Jesus to them in this way:

> You know of Jesus of Nazareth, how *God anointed Him with the Holy Spirit and with power*, and how He went about doing good and healing all who were oppressed by the devil, for God was with Him. (Acts 10:38, emphasis added)

If the anointing of the Holy Spirit was relevant for Jesus, how much more do we need it, if we take seriously the call to battle against the spiritual forces of evil that hold people in bondage? We will not experience victory in the battle unless we have all the power of God at our disposal.

Even before Jesus' public ministry began, John the Baptist preached the baptism of the Holy Spirit: "I baptized you with water; but He [Jesus] will baptize you with the Holy Spirit" (Mark 1:8). In

Jesus' last conversation with His disciples, He assured them that He would send the promise of the Father upon them, and that they would be "clothed with power from on high" (Luke 24:49). Both Acts 1:5 and Acts 11:16 cite the words of Jesus to His disciples, that they would receive the baptism of the Holy Spirit. As soon as this happened, the disciples went out with authority and power as witnesses of Jesus. Jesus said that those who receive the Spirit as a Helper will do even greater things than He had done[iv] (see John 14:12-17). The clear promise and pattern is that the Holy Spirit comes upon us in power, that we might do the works of Christ.

Even after years on the mission field, teaching, encouraging, fellowshipping, and trying to demonstrate the kingdom life with the guys, it often seemed like there were just some things they didn't understand. I have to admit my occasional frustration in this. Considering my neglect of the baptism of the Holy Spirit and my failure to emphasize His role in empowering believers for victory, I probably should not have been surprised. You can see the exact same thing happen in Jesus' own disciples. They walked with Jesus and were taught about the kingdom of God for over three years, but in so many things Jesus yet had to rebuke and re-teach them. They heard Jesus explicitly discuss His own death as the will of the Father, yet Peter went so far as to rebuke Jesus. And in spite of Jesus' teachings about not resisting evildoers and loving our enemies, Peter still struck the ear of the high priest's slave at Gethsemane when Jesus was being arrested (Matthew 26:51).

The ignorance and failings of Jesus' disciples should be understandable, if you acknowledge the absence of the Holy Spirit's filling and power. After all, Jesus said it is the Holy Spirit who would teach us and help us to remember all that He had said (John 14:26).

Likewise, even after spending several years training evangelists among the Kenyan brethren, I found that they lacked boldness to engage people at new locations. I expected that once equipped with knowledge, they would simply go out and do the work of making disciples that Jesus commanded in the Great Commission. I found myself frustrated by their lack of initiative and wondered why it was so.

Yet you can similarly see that after the death and resurrection of Jesus, the apostles were found in hiding, not sure what their next steps were to be. They certainly weren't out there sharing the good news. But Jesus had told them to tarry in the city for a specified purpose: "until you are clothed with power from on high" (Luke 24:49). Immediately after they received this promised gift, they were overwhelmed with boldness to preach and with power to do works in Jesus' name. If the apostles needed the baptism of the Holy Spirit to give them boldness in God's work, we certainly cannot expect to engage the enemy with any degree of courage or success under our own power.

It shouldn't surprise us, then, to see that the baptism of the Holy Spirit was given as a gift that is specifically designed to empower us for ministry. This was a clear pattern in Jesus' ministry and in the ministry of the apostles. Jesus said,

> "[Y]ou will receive power when the Holy Spirit has come upon you; and you shall be My witnesses both in Jerusalem, and in all Judea and Samaria, and even to the remotest part of the earth." (Acts 1:8)

But the work didn't stop with the apostles. The early church writings record similar activity for hundreds of years,[v] and it continues up to the present day. I was excited to see that after the Holy Spirit was invited into the Kenyan mission and the brethren were beginning to be baptized in the Spirit, they began to go forth of their own initiative to share the kingdom message and minister healing and deliverance. This was a very necessary development, and I was amazed that I had gone so long oblivious to the necessity of the Holy Spirit's work.

When you personally encounter God and receive His Spirit, it is not the end, but only the beginning. You must fan the flames in order to keep the fire burning. Imagine that a piece of charcoal is lit. This takes outside energy, which is the baptism of the Holy Spirit. The coal cannot stay lit by itself, but needs an updraft to keep it red-hot; this is the continued wind of the power of the Holy Spirit. If the coal is then piled together with other red-hot coals, the heat generated creates a self-perpetuating flame.

In the same way, the new, Spirit-filled believer must be in fellowship with other Spirit-filled believers to keep producing heat. The heat is the outward manifestations of the Spirit: power, revelations, and service. If we stop the flow of the Spirit or suppress His gifts, the coal will die.

Imagine that this red-hot coal is placed with a bunch of dead coals; it will either light the others or become smothered by them. A Spirit-filled believer in a dead fellowship either lights the fellowship with the flame of the Spirit or the believer himself grows cold.

Active engagement in the front-line battle is where we experience the ongoing work of the Holy Spirit and keep the fire of our fellowships lit. A church without evangelism and kingdom expansion is a dead church, indeed. It takes action and the ongoing work of the Holy Spirit to keep the embers burning. The gift of Pentecost—the fullness of the Holy Spirit—is not just for individual believers, but for the fellowship of the saints and for the expansion of God's kingdom.

No Christian would deny the work of the Holy Spirit, but I think the tendency is to limit His role and conform it to our understanding or experience. We would all acknowledge that the Holy Spirit convicts us of sin in regard to our salvation, leads us to confess Jesus as the Christ, and acts as a seal of our redemption at rebirth (see Ephesians 1:13 and 4:30, and 2 Corinthians 1:22). Yet there is still more: the baptism of the Holy Spirit, and then subsequent *fillings* with the Spirit (see, for example, Acts 4:8, 4:31, 13:9 and 13:52). It makes sense that the Holy Spirit would be available to *continually* fill us to overflowing so that we can serve the Lord in power and with boldness (Ephesians 5:18). After all, the promise of the Father is that rivers of living water will well up from within us (John 7:38). Living water is constantly flowing: emptying and filling, being poured out and replenished yet again.

You can see all of these functions of the Holy Spirit fulfilled in the experience of the apostle Peter. He was convicted of his sin by the Holy Spirit at the miraculous encounter with Jesus (Luke 5:8), he had faith in Jesus as the Christ at a later time by the same Spirit (John 16:8), then Jesus breathed into Peter and the others to "receive the Holy Spirit" after His resurrection (presumably as a seal of his salvation, as it was prior to Pentecost, see John 20:22). But that was not the end of his encounters with the Holy Spirit. Peter and the multitude were baptized with the Spirit at Pentecost and later, he was again filled with the Holy Spirit when the believers gathered in prayer. They had asked the Lord for continued courage and power, and in response, "the place where they had gathered together was shaken, and they were all filled with the Holy Spirit" (Acts 4:30).

Not everyone denies the baptism of the Holy Spirit, but many argue that this experience was limited to the apostles. On the contrary, we see throughout the book of Acts that people beyond the twelve apostles had such an experience (see Acts 9:17-18 and Acts 19:6, for example). Mark 16:17-18 is clearly addressed to *all* saints and references several gifts that can only be manifested through the power of the Holy Spirit. And the early church accepted this teaching even until the end of the fourth century.[vi]

> "Now these signs shall follow them that have believed in my name: they shall cast out devils; they shall speak with new tongues; they shall take up serpents; and if they drink any deadly thing, it shall by no means hurt them: they shall lay their hands on the sick, and they shall recover." These gifts were first bestowed on us the apostles when we were about to preach the gospel to every creature, and afterwards were of necessity

afforded to those who had by our means believed. (*Apostolic Constitutions[1]*. ANF v. 7, 479. Compiled c. 390 AD)

Likewise, 1 Corinthians chapters 12-14 were addressed to all the saints;[vii] Paul encouraged *all* the believers to "eagerly seek" the spiritual gifts. He also warned them not to forbid the speaking in tongues. If we continually see the gifts and the work of the Holy Spirit in the early church, we can conclude that this is something that is available to everyone, even today.

Perhaps the work of the Holy Spirit and the gifts were only for a time, and now they have been phased out—that's the next logical argument, right? The classic defense for this position is that (per 1 Corinthians 13:8-10) "perfection" has come, in the form of the canon of Scripture. However, the early church viewed "perfection" as referring to none other than the second advent of Christ, which is the most straightforward and logical interpretation.[viii] If perfection is already here, that means the war is over—the kingdom is established on Earth the way it is in Heaven and the enemy is defeated. That's a stretch, to say the least. Just as the apostles and the early church needed the ongoing work and fullness of the Holy Spirit, so do we today. And they continued to operate in ALL the gifts of the Holy Spirit for hundreds of years after the death of the apostles.[ix, x]

In Kenya, they eat a staple of boiled cornmeal call *ugali*. It is like grainy mashed potatoes eaten with their hands. I know it is not very appetizing to us Westerners, but they love it, and eat as much as they can every day. In fact, ask just about anyone and they'll tell you that their goal is to eat enough *ugali* at supper time that they can just drink tea for breakfast and still feel full until their late-afternoon lunch. So I ask them, "Would you just take one bite of *ugali* if you had it in front of you, or would you eat until you are full?" They unanimously say they want to be full. It is the same with the Holy Spirit. The early church understood Jesus to have the Holy Spirit "full and entire, not maimed in any measure or portion,"[xi] (see also John 3:34) and the apostles possessed the Holy Spirit "properly and fully,"[xii] whereas "ordinary" Christians experienced the Holy Spirit in a lesser measure. Yet I believe the greater measure is available to all of us if we empty ourselves of competing influences.

Convincing my African brethren who had been baptized years prior that they could still be lacking something spiritually took some

---

[1] Although the authorship of the *Apostolic Constitutions* is disputed among scholars, the writings still serve as a good representation of what the church believed at the time of its writing and compilation.

teaching. Yet I did not argue that their repentance or baptisms were invalid—I just urged them to seek and receive even more of the Holy Spirit. It was helpful that there were a couple of examples in the Bible of people doing exactly what we did. Philip, a deacon-turned-evangelist, traveled to Samaria, where he preached the kingdom, healed the sick, and expelled demons, even baptizing the first saints there. Yet for some reason, the Jerusalem church sent the apostles Peter and John to visit him there. They came and laid hands on the new saints so they would be baptized in the Holy Spirit (see Acts 8:4-24).

I personally believe that Philip, having been filled with the Holy Spirit himself (Acts 6:3), could have done it on his own. After all, we see that other disciples (beyond the twelve apostles) did the work of laying-on of hands elsewhere in Scripture, as when Ananias filled Saul with the Holy Spirit (Acts 9:17). Perhaps at that time, Philip was simply lacking in understanding or experience.

We find another account of post-baptism laying on of hands in Acts 19:1-7, when Paul inquired of some disciples in Ephesus, "Did you receive the Holy Spirit when you believed?" He discovered that they had received the baptism of repentance (baptism in water for forgiveness of sins) but after further teaching, he laid hands on them and they received the Holy Spirit as well. These examples made a good case for revisiting our brethren with the laying on of hands for the receiving of the Holy Spirit.

Of course, when we had baptized new brethren in the early years of our mission, we had prayed for them to receive the Holy Spirit, as do many Christian denominations today. However, it was lip-service only. There was certainly no dramatic evidence of people receiving the Holy Spirit, such as what Simon the Sorcerer must have seen in Samaria. Whatever he saw convinced him to try to *purchase* this gift. But what did we see? A whole lot of nothing! If Paul had asked us if we had received the Holy Spirit when we believed, we probably would have said, "Well of course. We prayed for it—and isn't it automatic?" But no one felt or saw anything. It was intellectual and theoretical only, with no experience to back up the claim.

When the Holy Spirit fell at Pentecost, Caesarea, Samaria, and Ephesus, everyone saw something and recognized that a work had been accomplished. The power of the Holy Spirit was also evident in the believers who went out preaching with boldness and confirming the message with signs and wonders. This was certainly not our experience. We were simply naïve in assuming that something had occurred. We are not making that mistake anymore. Before baptism, we teach not only the gospel of the kingdom but also the expectation of the impartation of the Holy Spirit at water baptism upon repentance. As we baptize, we pray in faith for the Holy Spirit to come with the laying on of hands and persist until His presence manifests (more on that in the next chapter). Now that we have repented of our neglect, we see people being baptized, filled, and empowered as soldiers on the front lines of the spiritual battle against the forces of darkness—and it is a battle in which *every* man is called to be equipped and engaged.

Chapter 4—Equipping the Soldiers

It was a Wednesday afternoon, shortly after Titus and Christine were filled with the Holy Spirit; wanting to continue the movement of God, I organized another visit with Pastor John, this time with four disciples. In attendance were a young man from our Kitale home fellowship named Frank, a married mother of six from our village, and two brethren from our Kapenguria fellowship. This time, we started with very few teachings, as I had prepared the brethren before the meeting with the biblical case for the baptism of the Holy Spirit. I also encouraged them to fast and pray, and to empty themselves of anything that would hinder the filling of the Spirit. Frank and Anna had fasted and really sought the Lord prior to the meeting; the Kapenguria brothers, unfortunately, had not.

We lifted our voices in praise, and with no effort on our part, Frank was baptized in the Holy Spirit and began speaking in tongues. We prayed for Anna...same result. She was overwhelmed by the Holy Spirit, even with her toddler clinging to her leg, and began speaking in tongues. Our focus shifted to the Kapenguria brethren: Justin— nothing. No movement whatsoever. He moved on to William with the same result. Those two young men unfortunately went home defeated in their desire to be filled with the Holy Spirit. Though fasting and prayer do not guarantee that the baptism of the Holy Spirit will occur, I do think that a certain level of spiritual preparedness assists in the process.

Immediately after this meeting, at about 5 PM, Anna and Christine left to attend a burial—these are big, community events that few will miss. On their way, they happened by the compound of Mama Michelle, a local widow from our fellowship. Mama Michelle is a wonderful old woman whom we all love dearly, but thus far, she hadn't seemed very serious about the faith.

Mama Michelle was, at the time, quite ill and needed prayer. The night before, she had received a dream that two mamas would visit her the next day to pray for her; as Anna and Christine passed, she thought to herself, *Here they are.* The young women, newly filled with the Holy Spirit and with boldness, were eager to pray for her. They had barely begun when Mama Michelle fell to the ground in deep repentance, sobbing uncontrollably. And without even having a hand laid on her, Mama Michelle was filled with the Holy Spirit and began to speak in tongues. The young ladies were amazed. God had begun something new among the brethren, indeed.

From my experience thus far, I have seen that it takes three things in order for a disciple to receive the baptism of the Holy Spirit: they must *believe*, they must *want it*, and they must proactively *get it*. The biblical basis for the baptism of the Holy Spirit in the last chapter was designed to help you believe that it is available to you. It is my hope that these testimonies will encourage you to want it. The next step is to equip you to go and get it. So stay with me.

Imagine if your father rented you a one-room studio apartment. After moving into the place, an acquaintance visits and starts spending the night there on your couch. He is not a particularly wholesome fellow. He drinks, uses recreational drugs, is up late welcoming friends (even prostitutes), and playing worldly music. He will not work; he eats all your food but contributes nothing towards the household expenses. Of course, ultimately you are very uncomfortable with his presence, yet you don't know how to confront the situation or get him to leave. So, you simply begin to make yourself scarce. Eventually, you find yourself either staying with others or coming to your own place only to sleep. It looks like your unwelcome visitor has found himself a cushy existence.

Now let's say the Holy Spirit is the lawful resident of that studio apartment, invited to live there by the Father. *We* become that "apartment" when we surrender to Christ in repentance—the Holy Spirit indwells us. Yet consider His very name; He is the *Holy* Spirit. How do you think He responds when we fill His place with all manner of evil and take advantage of His grace? We can see this analogy reflected in 1 Corinthians 6:19-21:

> Or do you not know that your body is a temple of the Holy Spirit who is in you, whom you have from God, and that you are not your own? For you have been bought with a price: therefore glorify God in your body.

The Holy Spirit jealously yearns for all of us (James 4:5). He does not want to share us with anyone. When He is forced to share the temple of our body with competing thoughts, activities, or spirits, He is grieved and made uncomfortable and makes Himself scarce.

The Shepherd of Hermas, a document written in the middle of the second century and very respected by the early church, sheds light on this very issue:

> "Be patient," said he, "and of good understanding, and you will rule over every wicked work, and you will work all righteousness. For if you be patient, the Holy Spirit that dwells in you will be pure. He will not be darkened by any evil spirit, but, dwelling in a broad region, he will rejoice and be glad; and with the vessel in which he dwells he will serve God in gladness, having great peace within himself. But if any outburst of anger take place, forthwith the Holy Spirit, who is tender, is straitened, not having a pure place, and He seeks to depart. For he is choked by the vile

spirit, and cannot attend on the Lord as he wishes, for anger pollutes him. For the Lord dwells in long-suffering, but the devil in anger. The two spirits, then, when dwelling in the same habitation, are at discord with each other, and are troublesome to that man in whom they dwell...For all these things are foolish and empty and unprofitable to the servants of God. But patience is great, and mighty, and strong, and calm in the midst of great enlargement, joyful, rejoicing, free from care, glorifying God at all times, having no bitterness in her, and abiding continually meek and quiet. Now this patience dwells with those who have complete faith. But anger is foolish, and fickle, and senseless. Now, of folly is begotten bitterness, and of bitterness anger, and of anger frenzy. This frenzy, the product of so many evils, ends in great and incurable sin. For when all these spirits dwell in one vessel in which the Holy Spirit also dwells, the vessel cannot contain them, but overflows. The tender Spirit, then, not being accustomed to dwell with the wicked spirit, nor with hardness, withdraws from such a man, and seeks to dwell with meekness and peacefulness. Then, when he withdraws from the man in whom he dwelt, the man is emptied of the righteous Spirit; and being henceforward filled with evil spirits, he is in a state of anarchy in every action, being dragged hither and thither by the evil spirits, and there is a complete darkness in his mind as to everything good. This, then, is what happens to all the angry. Wherefore do you depart from that most wicked spirit anger, and put on patience, and resist anger and bitterness, and you will be found in company with the purity which is loved by the Lord." (*Shepherd of Hermas. ANF* v. 2, 23. c. 150 AD)

The examples of our four brethren who were seeking the Holy Spirit show that those who consecrated themselves through fasting and prayer received more of His presence, but those who did not prepare a place for Him went home empty. Yet the quotes from *The Shepherd of Hermas* show that even in the time of the early church, there was an understanding that the baptism of the Holy Spirit wasn't "the end." We must also *maintain* the presence of the Holy Spirit by continually giving Him a worthy place of residence.

Let's begin with *receiving* the Holy Spirit. What can we do to assist in the process? Peter told the Jews on Pentecost,

"Repent, and each of you be baptized in the name of Jesus Christ for the forgiveness of your sins; and you will receive the gift of the Holy Spirit. For the promise is for you and your children and for all who are far off, as many as the Lord our God will call to Himself" (Acts 2:38-39).

Repentance and baptism are a prerequisite to receiving the baptism of the Holy Spirit. We see a single exception to this rule when Cornelius and his companions received the Holy Spirit prior to water baptism. However, this was a unique event that God used to demonstrate that salvation through Christ was being made available to the Gentiles. Though I have also seen people filled with the Spirit before water baptism, I always pursue the normative of water baptism first. Also note that this promise and gift is for *all* generations, as many as God will call. This was not something meant to end with the apostles, for the promise was also for successive generations of disciples.

Though you may have heard the words *repent* and *repentance*, it's important to really grasp their meaning. Recall I said that one of the purposes of this book was to expose the enemy's plans? One of the best ways he renders us ineffective and unproductive is by obscuring the truth just enough that we fail to enter into all that God intends for us. It begins at the beginning: with the call to repentance.

Satan enslaves us and binds us in three specific ways: the first, our sin; the second, our spiritual strongholds; and the third, unforgiveness. When those three chains are severed, we are free from his presence and power and our vessel is thus completely cleansed and made available for the filling of the Holy Spirit. As mentioned in the last chapter, I'm *not* saying that the Holy Spirit is absent entirely in the disciple who is not Spirit-baptized. Remember, it is the Holy Spirit who convicts of sin, it is He who brings us to believe in Christ as Savior, and it is He who seals us upon regeneration. However, I hope it is now clear that He may not possess all of us if we still cling to competing spirits or have not completely emptied ourselves so that He may fill us. This is accomplished, first, through repentance.

Humility is the heart of repentance: submitting to God, drawing near to Him, and desiring above all else to be cleansed and purified for His indwelling (see James 4:6-10). As you can see through my testimony and the stories of some of the brethren, fasting is an ideal way to deny the flesh and our selfish desires so that we can approach God in a pure way. As we come closer to God, any sins, competing spirits, or other forms of bondage are much more easily recognized. And in the midst of fasting, we see our Father for who He is and in stark contrast, we see ourselves for the desperately needy and deficient beings we are. Seeing ourselves compared to our God brings us to our knees; then truly, we are ready—ready for God to fill us with His promised gift.

In the Lord's Prayer, of all places, we find instructions for waging spiritual warfare as a prelude to receiving the gift of the Holy Spirit. Take a look:

> And he said unto them, When ye pray, say, Our Father which art in heaven, Hallowed be thy name. Thy kingdom come. Thy will be done, as in heaven, so in earth. Give us day by day our daily bread. And forgive us

our sins; for we also forgive every one that is indebted to us. And lead us not into temptation; but deliver us from evil (Luke 11:2-4 KJV).

It starts with glorifying the Father, then leads into a formal declaration of war: stating that the Father's kingdom will rule and reign on earth (that is, over Satan's kingdom), just as He rules and reigns in Heaven. Imagine how those two statements must irk the devil! We ask God to assist us with our practical daily need: food. Then we can see the breaking of the three chains that Satan binds us with: first, forgiveness for our sins is secured when we repent; the law of sin and death no longer applies, so that chain binding us to Satan is cut. Next, the command that we forgive those who have offended us. We are held in bondage as long as we are holding onto the wrongs done to us by others. Jesus said we can't be forgiven unless we also forgive. As we work our way through this prayer and are able to do as it says, we find chain number two cut. Lastly, keeping us from temptation and setting us free from the evil one. Do you see deliverance and freedom from strongholds? The third chain is broken. With the three chains cut, we are free. This cleansing opens the door for us to receive the Holy Spirit. It is not so much that we make ourselves "good enough" to receive this gift, but rather that as we empty ourselves, the Holy Spirit is given room to fill us.

Luke 11:5-13 shows us the way to approach God so that we might receive this promise. Jesus instructs us in the form of a parable—the story of a persistent man who goes to his friend in the night, explaining that he has unexpected company and needs three loaves of bread. The response? Basically, "We're all locked up and you woke us up from sleep. Go away!" But the guy just won't give up; so eventually he leaves with what he asked for.

In the same way, Jesus says that if we want to receive the good gift of the Holy Spirit, we must be persistent: ask, seek, and knock, until we gain our desire. And we can rest assured that if we are asking for something good—such as the Holy Spirit—He will not give us something less: not a snake for a fish, not a scorpion for an egg. Not an alternative spirit—something evil or demonic—if you are requesting that good gift which He, Himself, promised. He will give you what you seek: the baptism of the Holy Spirit.

I was alone in my living room, still a young Christian struggling to understand and experience this baptism of the Holy Spirit. I prayed unceasingly this very passage. I asked; I sought; I knocked. I persisted and would not relent until the Father delivered His promise. It was not hypnotism or psychological trickery. I was alone. I was stubborn and would not permit some prophet or evangelist to lay hands on my head and try to convince me that the gibberish I saw others speaking was really the Holy Spirit. I knew this was a gift from the Father. I knew Jesus was at the right hand of the Father advocating for this promise to be given to His children. So I prayed. And then the miracle happened. The Lord delivered His promised gift to me. I felt the Spirit's overwhelming presence and began to speak in tongues. Jesus spoke the truth; His Father would not fail in delivering His promise.

So when it comes to every believer receiving this gift, let's put together what we've seen so far: personal cleansing through repentance and breaking those three chains that hold us in bondage to Satan is vital. This can be concurrent with, or after, water baptism. What does this actually look like in practice?

Fasting for some time lends itself to success in this process, as we humble ourselves and become more attuned to the presence of God. The fast could be only one day, but it could be more. Someone seeking the fullness of the Spirit can do this on their own (I'll call them a "candidate" for Spirit baptism, just for ease of reference going forward), or a mentor can guide the candidate. Either way, the process is pretty much the same.

I recommend opening with a prayer, asking God to do His work of revelation in the candidate by the Holy Spirit. Songs of worship, for me, create the right atmosphere for hearing from God; I believe that these not only disturb competing spirits, but also welcome the Holy Spirit. Then, formally (on paper) or informally (through conversation or personal prayer), itemize what God reveals to the candidate regarding past sins, personal and family strongholds, and areas of victimization that lead to unforgiveness, anger, or bitterness: the three chains that Satan binds us with. Confession of and repentance for sins naturally follows, along with a prayer asking for God's forgiveness through the blood of Jesus Christ. Chain one is cut. Then, the candidate should verbally (authoritatively) declare allegiance to Christ and His kingdom and renounce Satan's claim on all recognized sins and strongholds. This should include a command for all unclean spirits to leave, if any have been identified. Chain number two, broken. Lastly, the candidate should recollect all areas of victimization (specific ways others have hurt them). One by one, sincerely forgive those who have abused, slandered, or hurt them in any way. It helps to recognize that the perpetrators are not the enemy, but rather are victims themselves of the real enemy, Satan. Then, the candidate will pray to break Satan's last chain.

If a mentor is involved in the process, he should now take over, praying nearly the same things over again, with eyes wide open, watching attentively for any manifestations of demons. If present, they can be expelled by command through the authority given by Christ. If not, just pray as if they are present and renounce their work.

We'll return to a discussion of demons in later chapters, but for now just be aware that spirits (personal and impersonal) and even sicknesses, all respond in the same way to authoritative prayers in the name of Jesus Christ; simply, they obey.[xiii] Therefore, treat them all the same. This is the time for deliverance.

If the candidate has not yet been baptized, he is now prepared for this step. Baptize him, laying on hands and petitioning the Father. Ask, seek, knock until the Holy Spirit is sent. You might advise the candidate to breathe in, and simply receive Him, as Jesus modeled. When His presence is sensed, tell them to speak—not their language, but as the Spirit gives utterance. Speaking in tongues is normal, but does not always happen when receiving the baptism of the Holy Spirit. That is often because we expect it to happen with no effort on our part. Sometimes, this is the case. But more often than not, some cooperation is required. The Holy Spirit provides the language, not the speaking. The candidate may need to begin by opening his mouth, or making some sounds, before the Holy Spirit imparts the speech.

Some people experience impediments to receiving the baptism of the Holy Spirit (for example, shyness, ignorance of how it's supposed to happen, etc.) and are hindered in speaking in tongues. Yet they often report feeling "warmth" in their belly, or (if they have their hands raised), a tingling movement down the arms, or an overwhelming feeling of joy. Don't relent in prayer until the Holy Spirit manifests in some way.

If there is no evidence of the baptism of the Holy Spirit, review the candidate's repentance and ask if there is anything else they need to repent for or if they feel that they are still in bondage in any area of their life. Note that unbelief and fear are strongholds that require confession, repentance, and renouncing. Those little devils are powerful to prevent Spirit baptism.

You may have noticed the element of "laying on of hands" in imparting the Holy Spirit (either during water baptism or separately afterwards). This is a biblical practice, in fact labeled as one of several "elementary teachings" in Hebrews 6:1-3. I see three distinct purposes for the laying on of hands in Scripture. One is ordaining church leadership, and a second is for the purpose of healing. Yet the third—imparting the baptism of the Holy Spirit—was actually the most visible of the three in the New Testament, specifically the book of Acts. Rather than cite the many examples (some of which have already been mentioned previously), I encourage you to take a quick read-through of the book of Acts. The number of mentions of the laying-on of hands for the baptism of the Holy Spirit may surprise you. Thus, I believe that the laying on of hands referenced in Hebrews (coupled, as it is, with the "elementary teachings" of repentance and baptism) refers to the baptism of the Holy Spirit. It is good practice, therefore, to make this part of receiving the baptism of the Holy Spirit.

So I've mentioned "speaking in tongues" as a part of receiving this promised gift. How did you react? Unfortunately, speaking in tongues as a result of Holy Spirit baptism is another one of those misunderstood and oft-debated topics, so as much as I would love to have the Scriptures speak for themselves and leave it at that, it's probably necessary to explore this topic a bit more in-depth.

First of all, Jesus Himself said that those who believe would speak in new tongues (Mark 16:17). Of course, the brethren who received the Holy Spirit at Pentecost spoke in tongues—actually, we see that they spoke strangely yet people understood them in their native language. That was a very unique event not repeated again in Scripture. The early church even endorsed the gift of tongues as from God.[xiv]

When Peter and John laid hands on the new disciples in Samaria, Simon the sorcerer saw that the brethren were receiving the Holy Spirit with the laying on of hands and sought to purchase that power (Acts 8:18-19). Now what exactly did Simon see that was so convincing that he was willing to part with money to receive it? Though the text is silent, I postulate they must have shown *evidence* of their Spirit baptism, elsewhere in Scripture being defined as the speaking in tongues.

Yet another example is Paul's healing and baptism by Ananias (Acts 9:17). Again, the text does not explicitly state that Paul spoke in tongues, yet in the letter to the Corinthian church he said that he spoke in tongues more than anyone (1 Corinthians 14:18). We can presume that he received that gift when he received the Holy Spirit.

When Peter ministered to the Gentiles, Cornelius and his companions spoke in tongues when receiving the baptism of the Holy Spirit (Acts 10:46). Paul Spirit-baptized the Ephesian saints, and all twelve spoke in tongues (Acts 19:6). As we examine the biblical examples of people receiving the Holy Spirit, almost all of them spoke in tongues; that is the overwhelming pattern and expectation from the Scriptures.

Paul further defines the speaking of tongues for the church in Corinth; he says that it is the Spirit in us petitioning to our God. The Spirit speaks mysteries that no man understands (1 Corinthians 14:2). Throughout this chapter, it is apparent that the "tongues" spoken of by Paul is an unintelligible spiritual language, intended for our God. Elsewhere he says that we often do not know what to pray, but the Spirit intercedes on our behalf with groaning too deep for words (Romans 8:26). Many have therefore said that the gift of tongues is simply a prayer language.

Paul clearly says not all speak in tongues. But he also says that we should not *forbid* the speaking in tongues. He says it is a "lesser" gift because it does not edify the body. It is an upward gift, towards God, and not a downward gift, towards man—that is, unless you have someone present with the gift of interpretation. Therefore, Paul restricts the speaking in tongues in a public service to times of sharing and edification, where the participants should be limited in number, orderly, and seek interpretation.

However, in most interactive fellowship services, there are times of prayer in which all are encouraged to participate, both silently and aloud. Personally, I believe that corporate prayer time is best done with everyone praying together in unity (more prayer, more power), though there are times when only one person will pray. Yet churches that insist on people praying one-by-one, especially if that person is specially selected, miss the entire point of Jesus' teaching that we should not pray with many words, just for others to hear. Prayer is for God to hear, and if He has given us a "prayer language," there's not a much better time to use it than when we come together to appeal to our God.

As if there weren't enough topics for debate, the idea that any of this activity of the Holy Spirit ceased with the apostles, or with the formalization of the canon, is just one more. Truthfully, I believe that this lie is the most effective strategy Satan has ever used to neuter the church. With one fell swoop, he took away all the tools available to the saints for attacking the powers of darkness. A careful study of the early church (specifically, the book of Acts, but also in the Ante-Nicene writings of the first few centuries) clearly shows that the saints continued to operate in the power of the Holy Spirit.[xv] The gifts may have diminished with time—in fact, in his writings of the third century, Origen actually mentions this and explains why. It was not that the Holy Spirit had changed; instead, the saints did:

> Moreover, the Holy Spirit gave signs of His presence at the beginning of Christ's ministry, and after His ascension He gave still more; but since that time these signs have diminished, although there are still traces of His presence in a few who have had their souls purified by the gospel, and their actions regulated by its influence. "For the holy Spirit of discipline will flee deceit, and remove from thoughts that are without understanding." (Origen, ANF v. 4, 615. c. 248)

Origen discerned that the Holy Spirit was more active among those whose life and walk was pure; like the writings in *The Shepherd of Hermas* that acknowledge the sensitivity of the Holy Spirit, Origen also taught that the Spirit would remove Himself from one who did not provide Him with a holy abode. Perhaps as Christianity moved farther and farther from the time of Christ and believers expected less, received less, and conformed more to the world, the Holy Spirit diminished in His activities. Yet, in Origen's day, He was still quite active. [xvi]

The inverse of this also holds true: those who are pure and full of understanding can, indeed, operate in the power and leading of the Holy Spirit. It is Satan's plan, his ultimate deceit, to lull us into powerlessness and complacency with his lie that the gifts have ceased. Anyone who wants to be engaged on the front lines against our spiritual enemy needs to be equipped with the truth: the impartation of the Holy Spirit and all of His power are absolutely necessary for engagement and, ultimately, victory.

God, Christ, and the Holy Spirit have not changed—*we* have. And we need to come back to trusting the Scriptures at face value. The early church believed the Holy Spirit was sent for the work of the last days, and clearly we are closer to the last days than they. [xvii] We must be honest with ourselves. If we picked up the Scriptures in a vacuum, with absolutely no outside influence or teachings, would we ever adopt the convoluted arguments which conclude that the gifts of the Spirit have ceased? Honestly, I don't believe so. Jesus said the learned would miss the kingdom, but that the humble and simple would find it. Don't believe the lies and deny God's promised gift.

You have to answer the question for yourself: "Did you receive the Holy Spirit when you believed?" If you see you are lacking and desire more, you simply need to believe in it, want it, and get it. I've given you some guidance, but if you need a boost of faith, I encourage you to find a Spirit-filled brother to assist you. Get the promised gift of the Father.

Chapter 5—Divine Healing in the King's Name

"Get up and walk!" I exclaimed, propelled by the excitement of seeing the woman's paralyzed leg move under her own power. Titus helped her to her feet and braced her by her arm as she walked for the first time in years.

I had learned about Stephanie through her daughter, Lydia, who was a waitress at our favorite restaurant in town. Upon Lydia's return to work from an extended absence, I asked her where she had been. She told me that she had been forced to take leave from work in order to stay at home and help her invalid mother. I inquired about her condition and she shared that Stephanie had suffered a stroke years back, rendering the entire left side of her body completely paralyzed. I asked if I could visit one day to pray for her healing. Lydia was thrilled, though I think she assumed the missionary would simply be a potential sponsor for further treatment.

A week later I visited Stephanie with a couple of our Spirit-filled brethren. We prayed, and she noted that all her pain went away. Then, after more prayer, she twitched her leg upwards just once and was able to physically twitch several fingers. When we followed up with her later, she reported that after that day, her anxiety and restlessness had also gone, allowing her restful sleep for the first time in a long time. These were not "pick up your mat and walk" reports, but we were pleased with measurable progress. The idea of healing by the authority of Jesus, as an expectation for *all* believers, was somewhat new to us, so even these small improvements following prayer were a real boost to our faith, and we promised her we would return.

On our follow-up visit, we gathered around Stephanie, opened with a couple of songs, and invited the Holy Spirit to do His work. On our previous visit, I had noted a bracelet that might be an invitation for something unclean. Upon my request, she removed it and I prayed against any unclean spirits. I then stepped up to pray against her paralysis, but after three honest tries, I backed down, defeated. Titus took over, and he wasn't going to give up so easily. He persevered in prayer for several minutes. And, suddenly, Stephanie was able to lift her leg—again, and again. We were amazed. God had done it!

That is when I told her to get up and walk. Completely under her own power, she walked around the room with Titus's support. She continues to gain strength and walk further and further to this day.

I still had many questions about divine healing at this point, and I was making many mistakes. However, God continued to show up in power to build my faith and experience sufficiently to press forward. I am so thankful that He did not give up on me.

It is my hope that through these stories, examples, and teachings, you can get a jump-start on what has taken me far too long to learn. Although you may not yet understand the significance of healing as a weapon in your arsenal against all the work of the enemy, it is certainly a means by which God shows forth His glory, persuades people of His presence, and frees people from their physical bondage.

One thing I have learned is that, when it comes to healing, our faith works along with God's power. As Jesus said, "According to your faith will it be done to you" (Matthew 9:29). We must believe what we do not see if we have any expectation of success in healing. And though at the time of my meeting with Stephanie I was still new to the inner workings of healing, God had certainly built my faith over my many years as a Christian, particularly to have confidence in Him for healing power. Without this foundation, I'm sure things would have progressed much more slowly for me.

My first experience with divine healing was in 2001. I was in a labor and delivery room with my wife and family members. I had just hung up the phone after receiving a grim report from a medical professional from the University hospital after a day of testing and evaluation on my newborn son. Jonah had a congenital diaphragmatic hernia—a hole in his diaphragm which had allowed his abdominal organs to be pushed into his lung cavity. That much we had already learned just a short time after his birth. But according to these updated reports, it got worse—a lot worse. His spleen was missing. His left kidney was not there. His entire small intestines were in his lung cavity and though he was full term, his lungs were under-developed. His heart was pushed to the right side of his body. His heart valves were not functioning properly and blood would not divert to the lungs but continued to flow to the umbilical cord. *Oh dear, this is serious*, I thought to myself.

I asked the woman on the other end of the line what his chances were. She said, in her opinion, he could not survive in his condition. I relayed the information immediately to the eagerly listening family who had gathered in the room with me (all but the terminal report). Though many family members responded with tears, Cindy and I felt oddly at peace—even confident. Some recent events in our lives gave us great faith in God's presence in this situation. Not the promise of a perfect outcome, but simply a promise of His perfect presence.

Shortly after, our pastor entered the room. We gave him the news, and he responded, "I've seen God work in things like this before." Under her breath, but audible enough for Cindy to catch, a crying family member muttered, "But He won't."

Months prior, as we had eagerly anticipated the birth of our second child, Cindy noted the development of a hernia, a condition which had affected her first labor and delivery, ultimately necessitating a C-section. I'll spare you the details, but I will say it was not the best experience and certainly not something we wanted to repeat. So when Cindy again had a hernia with this second pregnancy, we prayed in earnest that it would be healed. During a special evening church service, a visiting evangelist and prophet prayed for Cindy and the healing manifested. Yet that was just the half of it. He also prophesied that Jonah would be used mightily by God, and Cindy was even baptized with the Holy Spirit that day.

Fast forward: on the day of Jonah's birth, I was out working on a project with a friend. This was back in the day before we had cell phones, so Cindy tried the landline but we were all in the barn, so those calls were left unanswered. When I finally arrived home, Cindy's contractions were close together, but we knew we still had time. I cleaned myself up and we went to the hospital. When we arrived, they said she was already eight centimeters dilated, so it was too late for meds. The labor was hard, but after a successful delivery, I cut the cord. All seemed fine. Jonah was 7 pounds, 12 ounces (our largest to date of nine). Then we noted concern on the faces of the hospital staff as Jonah remained blue for longer than expected. He clearly could not breathe on his own. He was rushed off before we even got a chance to hold him.

Information was slow in coming, but I pieced together what I could. I caught bits of conversation and was able to see a scan displaying an ominous black mass in the chest cavity. I knew my anatomy, and that was not right. I immediately telephoned my sister-in-law, who began the prayer chains. The hospital called in five doctors from neighboring hospitals to assess his condition. Then they came to give us the news: he had a congenital diaphragmatic hernia. I asked the doctor what was the best case scenario, and what was the worst. He said the best we could expect was surgery to move the organs and repair the hole in the diaphragm. If all went perfectly, Jonah might be home in three-to-six months, but he would likely have long-term care needs. The worst: he would not make it to, or through, surgery.

They brought Jonah to our room in a bubble, with a respirator and many wires and an IV, and allowed us to say goodbye. He would be immediately transported by ambulance to the University hospital that morning. We were never even given an opportunity to touch him. He was gone. And we were stuck in the maternity room of the hospital, completely uncertain of his future.

We were a bit relieved when, finally, we found ourselves alone. We both had an eerie, supernatural peace. I said, "If the God of the universe can keep me from a car accident, He is all over this Jonah thing." This was referring to a miracle that had occurred on my way to work just days earlier; I'll talk more about it later. But the event was still fresh in my mind at that time, and by it God had built my faith even for this moment.

Even after receiving the fuller report after more evaluation and sharing it with our friends and family, we found our peace unshaken. Though I didn't know exactly why at the time, I became certain that it was because of the sheer number of people praying for us; we would only find out later just how many were bringing our urgent need to the Father. I told Cindy, "Better this happened to us than someone else, because we are equipped to handle it." Truly, and almost without explanation, we were sincerely willing to accept whatever God gave us, without reservation or complaint. We trusted in Him to know best.

Then He said it—I heard in my spirit, "Because you are willing to accept whatever I give you, I will give you my best." Whoa! Could that mean Jonah would be completely healed? I recognized God's voice. He had prepared me for this just days earlier when he prevented me from being in a car wreck. He had trained me to be attentive to His voice and presence. And suddenly, again: "Just like you gave me the truck and all the parts were there and they all worked, it will be the same with Jonah. All the parts are there, and they all work." This referred back to another recent event in which I had seen the hand of God and felt His leading—another faith-builder occurring just when God knew I would need it most.

Elated in spite of the grim reality for which we were being prepared, we packed for home. We simply could not stay at a hospital while our boy was not even there. On the way home, while cresting a knoll on the highway, God spoke to me again. He said He does not do things halfway. Jonah would be completely healed. Full recovery. No side effects. I would go on to share this report with my wife, sister-in-law, and pastor only.

Now we were not only at peace, but eagerly anticipating God's amazing promise: the miracle of Jonah's healing. The doctors had scheduled the surgery days out, as he was stable on the ventilator and things did not seem urgent. But then, at 5 AM the next morning, the call came. They asked for our verbal approval to prep Jonah for immediate surgery. Though they did not specify what had happened, his condition was suddenly critical. For the very first time, it actually entered my mind that my son could die. It was real, primal fear like I had never experienced. I made just one phone call to my sister-in-law, and my faith in God's promise was restored.

We got ourselves ready to go to the hospital, but we were advised that there was no rush, as it was a very lengthy surgery. We arrived at the University hospital to find that the surgery had already been completed. It took us some time to find the surgeon in the giant labyrinth of a hospital. Eventually he emerged from a room with his surgical scrubs on and wore an enormous, ear-to-ear smile. He reported that Jonah's lungs were pink, not gray, meaning that they were properly developed. He said the spleen was found with the intestines in the lung cavity. Then, with much animation and fanfare, a look of seriousness and yet joyful amazement, he said, "I reached back with my pinky and I TOUCHED IT—THE KIDNEY. IT WAS THERE!" That sealed the deal for us. God's miracle. His promise to me. He did it! Our emotions soared to places unimaginable and impossible to put into words. Our son had been healed!

When my sister-in-law arrived at the hospital we could not help but notice the many red specks on her face, particularly around her eyes. To our shock, she had been interceding so fervently that many of the capillaries in her face had burst. She reported that she literally felt Jonah's incisions during the time of the surgery. The depths of God's riches are beyond our understanding.

Friends began visiting the hospital. We shared the news and a buzz of excitement surrounded us; so much joy, in fact, that one of the nurses pulled us aside into a private room and warned us that Jonah's condition was still critical and his recovery still uncertain. She meant well, but had no idea of the experiences we had been through.

Jonah's next move was to Boston Children's Hospital, several hours from our home. The local University hospital feared that they were not equipped for a turn for the worst, and wanted to have neonatal ECMO (a heart-lung machine) readily available. Once again, we said goodbye to our bubble baby and headed home.

When Jonah was just 11 days old, the Lord spoke to me for the final time during this season. He said, "It is finished. He is healed. It will just take the doctors some time to figure it out." Later that evening I received a call from the on-staff nurse, reporting that Jonah had undergone a sudden and remarkable change. He was alert, active, and pulling off all his tubes and wires. She said he had been transferred from the ICU and was being weaned off all meds. We were told we could come that Friday so Cindy could spend the night and give him his first bottle. However, she gave a stern disclaimer that Jonah may have lost his sucking reflex because of the ventilator and may also have digestion problems. But we knew better.

Jonah took his first, second, and every bottle thereafter with no problem whatsoever. He was discharged three weeks from the date of his birth, and has never experienced any negative side effects. That time period, three weeks, would become significant many years later when I was seriously injured in a motorcycle accident in Africa.

Once discharged, Jonah was examined at our home by a visiting nurse. She asked Cindy when his surgery had been. Cindy responded, "The eleventh."

She asked, "June?," as it was now early July. Cindy replied, "Yes," and asked her why.

She responded, "Because a colleague of mine takes care of a boy that had a congenital diaphragmatic hernia and he requires 18-hour-a day care, and your baby is doing so well." Cindy asked why the other boy was not still in the hospital. She answered, "Because he is in kindergarten. He is five years old." Suddenly aware once again of the gravity of Jonah's situation, Cindy was thankful to receive a clean bill of health for Jonah, with no follow-up visits from the nurse required.

We were humbled and amazed by God's personal intervention in our lives and the life of our son. Before that time, we saw God as somewhat distant and sterile—you know, the God of a book. After that event we realized that God was not trapped between the covers of a leather-bound. He is alive, active, still speaking and intervening personally in the lives of His children. Our lives were forever changed.

Though we had seen God heal our son, and He was definitely strengthening our faith to believe in Him for greater things, we still had glossed over the Scriptures that speak of the ability of *every* Christian to practice the laying on of hands for healing—not as a special gift, but simply because of the authority of Jesus and in His name. Jesus' name has a lot of power, as even the early church recognized.[xviii]

Mark 16:17-18 tells us the very words of Jesus:

> "These signs will accompany those who have believed: in My name they will cast out demons, they will speak with new tongues; they will pick up serpents, and if they drink any deadly poison, it will not hurt them; they will lay hands on the sick, and they will recover."

Some say these words can't be trusted since they are not in *all* the earliest manuscripts. Yet, they are present in every translation of the Bible available today, and we have already read these words from the *Apostolic Constitutions* (circa 390 AD) as applying to all Christians. Regardless of this historical precedent, some still say these words were only written to the apostles; however, when Jesus sent out the seventy, it was not limited to the small group of the twelve, or just to "apostles." Philip was named as a deacon, and he went out to heal the sick and expel demons. Ananias was "just another disciple," but he was chosen to go lay hands on Paul so that he could receive his sight after the Damascus Road experience with Christ. And what about Paul? He was not one of the twelve.

The early church witness also demonstrates that these activities persisted after the death of the apostles. If healings (and other works of the Spirit) were simply for the apostles present during the time of Jesus, we would not see them recorded as being accomplished by others, nor would we expect to see them referred to by the early church for normal Christians, yet we do.[xix] Just as with the baptism of the Holy Spirit, I believe that Satan wants to deny the work of healing as available to every believer, even to the present day, to take one more weapon out of our hands and strengthen his own position.

If these words of Jesus are not enough to convince you, Jesus promised that those who would believe in Him would not only do the works He had done, but even greater things (John 14:12). It is, therefore, reasonable to expect, and see, *miracles.*

Paul said that not all have the gift of healing. Yet Jesus said that those who believe *will* heal the sick. How do we reconcile these two seemingly conflicting statements?

Truthfully, for years I prayed for many people to be healed and saw only one here and there *actually* healed. But today, that the "one here and there" corresponds to the ones *not* healed. And keep in mind, I'm not out there doing this alone—my African brethren are just as active, and their experience is similar to mine. Yet none of us believes that we have the gift of healing. How can this be? It is all about *authority.*

Jesus commanded the twelve to preach the kingdom and heal the sick (Luke 9:2). And we see that they did just that: preached the kingdom and healed the sick. Do you suppose He would command them to do something that they were not capable of doing? Of course He would not.

Anyone who has children knows that you don't ask a two year-old to shovel a driveway full of snow; if you do, you'll surely be disappointed. But when you ask your sixteen year-old, you can expect that he will get out there and do the work, and do it well. In fact, if he does not, there will probably be consequences.

Likewise, when Jesus commanded His disciples, He expected them to obey, and He obviously felt that they were equipped with what they needed. Yet they were just fishermen and tradesmen, not particularly well-educated or skilled. Their ability to do such incredible work came directly from their Master: "[Jesus]...gave them *power* and *authority* over all the demons and to heal diseases" (Luke 9:1, emphasis added). Everything they needed was at their disposal.

Let's go back to our simple parenting example. Parents have the authority to command their children in certain things, like in asking them to help with household chores or shoveling the driveway. Yet they also must empower their children to accomplish those tasks, by starting simple when their skill level is low and working up to more difficult things. Training, encouragement, and patience are also required. Yet with time, we expect our children to successfully accomplish what is asked of them.

In the case of the apostles, with just a word, Jesus imparted to them everything they would need—both the power and the authority—to command demons and heal diseases. He also showed them by His example. With that equipping, He expected that they would go out and do the work.

Perhaps you wouldn't deny the impartation of this power and authority to the apostles. After all, they are like "super people," almost on par with Jesus Himself, in the eyes of most. Well, the very next chapter (Luke 10) documents Jesus sending out seventy others—that is, beyond the apostles—and commanding them to do the same exact work. Jubilantly, they reported upon their return that even the demons are subject to them in His name. Jesus again reminded them that He had given them authority over all the power of the enemy— implying that these results shouldn't have surprised them.

So how many of these men possessed the *gift* of healing? None of them did. The Holy Spirit had not yet been sent, thus none had received any of the gifts of the Spirit. How many of them healed people? I would guess *all* of them. How, then, were they able to heal the sick and expel demons without the power of the Holy Spirit? Simply by the authority of the name of Jesus. The name has power and is feared and obeyed.

Healing is possible apart from the gifting of the Holy Spirit, and we see that Jesus extended this power and authority to the seventy, beyond just the twelve. But what does this have to do with you and me?

Jesus' departing words to His followers, known as "The Great Commission" (Matthew 28:18-20), states that all power and authority in heaven and on earth rest with Him. He commanded the remaining eleven to make disciples, baptizing them, and "teaching them to observe all I have commanded you." Jesus expected that everything He had commanded the apostles would be passed on to successive generations of disciples. That, my friend, includes you and me. And just so you don't think this is a short-term promise, He assured them that He would be with them *always*, until the very end of the age, with all that power and authority to accomplish His works. We see in the early church testimony that they understood that the edict and authority given to the twelve, and specifically the seventy (Luke 10:19), were applicable to all Christians long after the death of the apostles.[xx]

Think about it this way: I tell my neighbor to take my motorcycle to the shop for an oil change. A friend sees my neighbor, someone who he does not know, driving my motorcycle in town and immediately accuses the neighbor of stealing my bike. The neighbor insists that I told him to take the motorbike in for an oil change, and he is therefore authorized to be riding it. The friend confirms the report with me by phone, and releases the neighbor to do the work without any further trouble.

The way *authority* works is that once someone is commanded to do something on behalf of the power behind the command, he immediately has the authority of that power to perform the task commanded. So we, as disciples of Christ, have been commanded to heal the sick and expel demons. In His name, we have that power and authority. Sicknesses and unclean spirits are subject to us in His name, by command.

The only thing Jesus ever marveled at was the centurion who understood the power of authority in healing (Matthew 8:5-13). When the centurion approached Jesus to ask for the healing of his servant, he humbly dissuaded Jesus from coming to his house to do the work. Instead, he told Jesus that as a soldier himself—one being under authority *and* having authority over others—he knew how things worked. He recognized Jesus' power and authority over sickness, so he told Him, "Just say the word, and my servant will be healed."

Jesus was impressed with this soldier's faith in His authority. Likewise, we are soldiers under authority, and we can use that authority as Jesus commands us (and therefore, permits us)—to heal the sick and cast out demons.

What was it that greatly disappointed Jesus? When the father of the sick lunatic came to Him complaining that the apostles could not heal and deliver him (Matthew 17:14-18), Jesus severely rebuked them: "You unbelieving and perverted generation, how long shall I be with you? How long shall I put up with you?" Then Jesus healed the boy Himself. The cultural Jesus of our imagination would probably have said, "Good try. Maybe next time you will succeed. You did your best." But that is not the *real* Jesus. The real Jesus demonstrated the work, He commanded them to perform the tasks, He equipped them, and He expected them to do it. In this case, Jesus was like an employer directing an employee to do a job, but then having a customer complain about the work. Being forced to do it Himself to please the customer, He was justifiably upset and disappointed with His workers.

Another example was when the disciples were in the boat and Jesus approached them walking on the sea (Matthew 14:24-31). Peter said to Him, "Lord, if it is You, command me to come to You on the water." Now why would Peter say such a thing? Well, I can only imagine that if Peter had impulsively gotten out of the boat and walked towards Jesus, he would have sunk like a stone! But when Jesus said, "Come," Peter was now *commanded* to come to Him on the water and had the authority to do so. Yet note what happened when Peter lost faith due to fear: unbelief resulted in failure. Peter's response was to cry out, "Lord, save me!" Jesus *did* save him, but also rebuked him for his doubt and little faith.

Now again, the Jesus of our imagination would simply commend Peter for stepping out onto the water. I mean, he was the only one who tried, right? But not the *real* Jesus. The real Jesus commanded Peter to come to Him, and therefore expected him to do just that. When he failed, Jesus was justifiably disappointed.

With the command, comes the authority to perform the task commanded, in the name of the commander. We are engaged in a very real spiritual battle, and must leverage all the power and authority at our disposal to advance the kingdom of God. We must operate in the faith of the centurion, not in the doubt of Peter, and believe that Jesus has fully equipped us to do this work on His behalf. Then, we must get out there and *do it*.

Chapter 6—Healing in the King's Service

"Healed? The X-ray said no fracture? A broken arm, really?" Wow! *Things have just gone to a new level*, I thought to myself.

Eric was approaching 70 years-old, but was still strong and active for his age, working daily to care for his wife and the grandchildren that had been abandoned to their care. Then he broke his arm, right near the wrist. Our mission assisted him with treatment and with his family's food needs during his recovery, but the arm mended slowly. Medical care in Kenya is hit-or-miss, entirely dependent on the attending doctor and not necessarily the hospital. I am not sure how good his care was, but it seemed to me that the cast was removed prematurely. During a checkup after the removal, the doctor stressed the broken arm to test it, and it broke again. Instead of recasting it, the doctor simply wrapped it in a bandage.

Months later, Eric was bringing food home for his family and was involved in a motorbike accident. In an attempt to break his fall, he snapped his arm again. It made a distinct *crack*, and the piercing pain and swelling were instant. He called brother Chris for help.

At the time, I was teaching eight of our strongest disciples, going through drill-and-practice field evangelism presentations. We were all gathered together in the prayer house in my Kenya compound when Chris took the call. I sensed the urgency and asked what was going on. Upon hearing the news, I told Isaiah to organize a medical escort and get Eric brought to us; from there, we would get him to a hospital for immediate treatment. I found out that *Mzee* Harold, the escort of choice for such a task, was already at the district hospital with another patient, so we just needed to send Eric to him with the necessary funds.

Eric arrived some 20 minutes later. Isaiah met him outside and gave him money and instructions to meet *Mzee* Harold. Almost as an afterthought, I asked Isaiah to send Eric in for prayer. I laid hands on the injury, which was clearly swollen and, based on Eric's reaction to my light touch, very painful. Several prayer warriors surrounded us, adding fuel to the fire. I prayed, seeking for the moment only to reduce or eliminate the obvious pain. Those types of healings were within my realm of experience. Never did I expect more. The pain was immediately relieved, so we praised God and sent Eric on his way. Our training session continued.

That evening *Mzee* Harold came to our home to settle the accounts, receipts, and change for the day's patients. He reported that when Eric had arrived at the hospital, the pain was still gone. Not only that, but the swelling had also disappeared. They proceeded with an

X-ray to assess the damage and see what treatment was required. There was no way it could *not* be broken. Yet upon review of the expected fracture, not a trace of breakage; it had been completely healed!

I was totally amazed. I knew that I had lacked sufficient faith to see a broken bone healed. However, Isaiah told me, "I thought it would be healed. Titus did, too." The faith to heal was present not in me, but cumulatively in the brethren surrounding me.

Healing is by the authority of the name of Jesus Christ. It is not just the work of the uniquely gifted or "anointed." It is the work of *all* Christians. James said when anyone is sick to call the elders of the church to pray for them in Jesus' name, and the prayer offered in faith will restore the sick person. He immediately made the point that the prayer of a righteous man is powerful and effective. He likewise clearly explained that Elijah was a normal man, just like us, but did extraordinary miracles, simply because he was a righteous man praying in faith (James 5:13-18). I repeat, healing is not just for special people, but for all saints. Yet sufficient faith is required as we pray. I want to offer you some hands-on advice on healing and hopefully activate *your* faith and motivate you to action.

If you don't believe healing is for today, or that you were commanded to heal and have the authority to do so, this chapter is not for you. Have you heard the expression *self-fulfilling prophecy*? Doubt, especially when it results from cessationist beliefs, is like that. You doubt things because you don't see them, yet according to God's paradigm ("according to your faith will it be done to you"), you will not see greater things if you don't bring faith into the equation. You must break through this stronghold if you are ever going to be used by God in demonstrations of power.

The first lesson in healing is a simple one: Do not ask God to do what He commanded *you* to do. Remember, when Peter yelled, "Save me!" Jesus rebuked him because He had already commanded him to come to Him on the water. Jesus already gave us the authority to heal all kinds of diseases. So, when you are operating under the authority of Jesus and in His name, don't pray to God or Jesus. *Command the sickness or injury* to go away. For example, "Headache, go away in the name of Jesus. I command all pain to go, *now*, in Jesus' name. Healed, in Jesus' name!" Combined with your faith, such authority in Jesus' name is sufficient for healing.

That is not to say that we cannot, or do not, pray to God. Of course we pray to God, but not on game day. A missionary mentor of mine shared some good advice that I've always remembered: *five hours of prayer for five minutes of power*. Though this is not a biblical teaching and the ratio is certainly not set in stone, the idea is that we can't go out expecting to see a movement of God if we haven't put in plenty of time in personal prayer, seeking God for the events we know we will encounter. Pray, pray, and pray some more *before* you go out in the field, so that His power will be upon you when you command those sicknesses to go away. But when facing a sickness or a demon, command it, rather than asking God to deal with it.

I treat sicknesses, injuries, pains, demons, and impersonal spirits all the same. I rebuke them, command them to leave, and bind them so they do not return. Why? Jesus gave us authority over all of these (Luke 9:1), and in the name of Jesus all of them obey identically.

Everyone will develop a different style of prayer that works for them. I would characterize mine as a more forceful and loud approach. Why? Because it has proven effective for me; my faith increased as I saw results doing it this way, so that is what I've stuck with. I've seen others that talk to illnesses very gently, and I'm almost surprised that those techniques work just as well for them.

Let's say my dog gets into a food cupboard. If I were to quietly say, "Go away, please stop" to my very motivated German Shepherd, he would likely ignore me. Unfortunately, he is often more interested in food than in obedience. The only thing that produces a different result is if I raise my voice and speak authoritatively: "STOP! GO, NOW!" In fact, with this approach, the desired result is quite immediate. Since this is my expectation and my approach—because my faith is activated in believing this will work—this is also what works for me as an approach to healing prayer.

As you practice the laying on of hands for healing, you will develop a certain style. But remember, the power and authority of Jesus are sufficient for any issue or predicament we face, and I don't suppose Jesus ever needed to yell and scream. He advised us, in all of our actions, to be people of peace, not harshness or violence (Matthew 5:9). Likewise, as Paul discussed the manifestation of the gifts in the church, he taught that there should be order, "for God is not a God of confusion but of peace" (1 Corinthians 14:33). All of this should guide how we proceed in healing prayer.

Next lesson, demonstrated by the testimony of Eric's broken arm: faith is cumulative. It is not simply the faith of the person praying, but also the faith of the patient, the bystanders, and others praying. If there are many of you, all should pray at once to give a greater chance of success. Do not take turns; that was a mistake I used to make. However, it became obvious that if the first attempt failed, the faith in the room literally came down for all parties involved, and it was increasingly difficult for faith to manifest.

Successful healing (especially at first) also requires some evaluation and discernment on your part. If there is more than one person seeking healing, start with the least-difficult cases. Always pick ailments for which you have had prior success first. These you know you can do, and you already have sufficient faith. As these are addressed, the "faith reservoir" in the room will fill up, providing strength for those cases you may perceive as more challenging.

One day Titus and Isaiah were busy at our ministry office when a woman came looking for our deacon, seeking medical treatment for a sick child at her home. When they could not find Moses, the two young men offered to go pray for the child. She agreed. At her home, they found two children: one, about two years-old with the common malaria symptoms of diarrhea, vomiting, fever, and achiness; the second, an orphaned neighbor boy about 12 years-old, with similar issues. Starting with the older boy, Titus first prayed for the stomach ache; the boy quickly reported the pain leaving that area. He moved on to leg aches, then headache, and finally the fever. As he progressed, the ailments took several attempts; however, Titus did not move on to the next symptom until the first ones were relieved. Slow and steady, he addressed one thing at a time. When each individual symptom was healed, Titus prayed for the malaria itself, and the boy reported full healing. Isaiah then prayed for the young child just twice, and he also was healed.

The next day, the older boy visited Titus and Isaiah at our compound and reported that he felt great, except that the headache returned. He did not come for medicine this time, but rather just for prayer. He believed. They prayed for his headache and it went away completely. He was totally healed of his malaria, as was the other boy.

The take-away here is to break big challenges into discrete parts. How do you eat an elephant? One bite at a time. So, for example, if you have an injury that is spread out over a limb, start with the foot. Then move on to the ankle, followed by the leg and hip. Or, ask some questions and work in order of increasing difficulty, one thing at a time. If you pray for a big, general healing, success requires far greater faith. But when you see progress on each discrete part, it adds to the faith reservoir and increases the likelihood for success. Isaiah was able to pray for the entire sickness at once for the second child because their faith reservoir was full, having just witnessed the first child being completely healed.

Perseverance in prayer is often required. Praying continuously can increase the likelihood of success, but only if you continue to have faith. Personally, I wimp out at three tries. If I don't see results, I simply give it to God. Maybe He will rebuke me later. But being an introvert, the embarrassment of continued failure totally deflates my faith and at that point, I really am not expecting results. Some of the brethren here can pray unceasingly, with complete confidence. They are able to add more and more faith to the challenge and chip away towards success.

If possible, always ask the patient to "test" the area of the problem immediately before and immediately after praying. Even if healing is not instant, many times patients will report discernable improvement upon prayer, which increases the faith to continue. Very often in such cases, complete healing will result ultimately. However, many people ask for prayer with absolutely no expectation of seeing results, and if you don't ask them right away how it feels, there might be no evidence of anything happening. In my experience, most healings occur *during* the checking, not before—so check immediately.

Recently, my son Jonah asked for prayer for a sore throat. He reported, almost surprised, "I was swallowing the whole time you prayed, just to see if it was getting better. But nothing at all happened until you asked me to swallow and see if it felt better—and that was when it went away completely." If the desired result is not achieved, continue to pray. Any and all improvement will add to the faith reservoir, which can enable you to finish the job.

As you are still growing in faith, you may not see significant results for big issues. You might need to settle for small improvements, as we did with Stephanie's paralysis: pain reduced, swelling gone—anything worthy of praise. Take what you can get. We are not Jesus. I do believe that all problems can be healed, and completely, *if* we have sufficient faith. But we don't have that faith out of the box. We need the faith *of* God, not faith *in* God—His power in us. But that kind of faith is built slowly. So be patient and look for measurable progress that can further encourage you for the next time. Discouragement is one of the most effective tools that Satan will use to immobilize you as you seek to grow in this area; don't let yourself fall prey to this particular tactic but rather, encourage yourself in the Lord.

Specifically, take on small challenges where you are comfortable. You may want to start with headaches and pains with family members (i.e., with your children, if you are a parent. Extended family may pose more of a challenge). Personally, though, I have seen better results with strangers than with friends and family. This is because I believe that God uses demonstrations of power for proclaiming His kingdom. See where your faith rests, and go from there to increase it.

As I grew more experienced in healing and began to share testimonies of what God was doing, I was surprised to get many requests for healing prayer via Facebook. One Facebook friend asked me via Messenger to pray for the strengthening of her husband, who had just recently begun to walk after having been paralyzed for 27 years. We picked a time for the next day because he was already in bed, but I prayed immediately anyway, since it was a convenient time for me. When he felt instant effects, they picked up our chat again to relay the incredible phenomena he was experiencing.

She asked me, "Are you praying now? His calf is burning and he said it feels like someone is pulling on his foot!"

I responded that, yes, I was praying for his left leg. I inquired about his second area of difficulty: "How about his abs?" She said, "No, but his leg is going up and down by itself and *whoa*, yes, his abs are burning now, too!"

I was sitting in our small back room, which contained two small shelves of books, two plastic chairs, a well-used coffee table, and an area rug. Needing a private place to pray, I had claimed it for my own use as needed. And remember what I said about my prayer style? It wasn't unusual for me to raise my voice and get *commanding* when anyone messaged or called with a prayer need.

In this case, I sat in the chair with my Messenger app open, commanding the leg to strengthen, the abs to strengthen, and the paralysis to desist. Yes, verbally, loudly, authoritatively—just as if the man was directly at my side and I was laying hands on him. The symptoms obeyed, regardless of the fact that we were separated by an ocean and thousands of miles. Evidently, the authority of Jesus' name knows no distance.

I would come to do things like this with several people via Messenger on multiple continents, with equally amazing results. For all those who say that faith healing by the authority of the name of Jesus is simply hypnotism or psychological tricks, you try telling that to the people who were healed in real-time and did not even know that I was praying—only to have me message to confirm their complete healing. The authority and power of the name of Jesus is only predicated on faith, not on proximity.

Some fear that such healings are simply the power of suggestion. Well, in a sense, they are—because ultimately, that is what faith is. When the woman touched Jesus' garment, when people walked under Peter's shadow or touched Paul's handkerchief, there was no inherent power in those objects, yet the people who sought healing had a certain level of faith in them. We have faith in the power and authority of the name of Jesus to heal. We eagerly expect such healing. If there is pain, we expect it to go. Sickness, we expect it to obey. Our faith can overcome many obstacles—including distance, as I learned.

"The woman with persistent bleeding healed, just like Jesus did. Wow!"

That was the report from Victor, the woman's neighbor, after I had come to their small fishing village with the gospel of the kingdom; this visit had been accompanied by various manifestations of God's power.

I had been to visit that particular group on several occasions, the number in attendance changing and growing each time. People were mostly coming in search of healing, but they had to sit through some lengthy teaching before we got to that.

Even the local Imam's relatives were there. At first, they had been forbidden. Yet when the 16-year-old son of the Imam begged his father, having exhausted all other hope for the healing of his badly infected leg, his father reluctantly permitted his ongoing attendance. Numerous others with various sicknesses came. The word had gotten out.

When the teaching concluded, I inquired as to the sicknesses. I registered them in my mental log and ordered them by level of difficulty. I had learned to start with the conditions for which I had prior success. As people are healed with the simple problems, the faith of the onlookers increased (as did mine), and more difficult cases began to yield success.

So first up, a woman with a headache. I prayed for her. Piece of cake, right? Nothing! *Oh dear.* That was not expected. I tried again. Again, no improvement. Bystanders began laughing and speaking in their local dialect. I was now deeply fearing failure on this first case. At this point, failure could seriously deflate me and crush the faith of everyone present, sabotaging the entire day's mission.

I was now determined. I looked intently at the woman and realized there was a spirit underlying the pain. I loudly and firmly commanded any spirit in this woman to leave and for all pain to go, immediately, in Jesus' name. I apprehensively asked how she felt: *"Please, please, please, Lord,"* I thought to myself, awaiting the response. Healed! Victory in Jesus!

Then everyone started moving in closer, "Me next, me!" I prayed for them one by one and all were immediately healed or saw remarkable improvement. God showed up. But one woman kept her distance. She pulled my translator aside and shyly confessed her ongoing vaginal bleeding, continuous for three months now. Matthew brought me the report and I called her to the center of the crowd. I put her hand on her abdomen and placed my hand over hers and discretely, without revealing the actual condition to the crowd, commanded the condition to go away. We closed the meeting with prayer and parted ways.

Not everyone can be verified as healed immediately when you pray. However, you must continue to believe, and lift those uncertain cases up to God during your private prayer time, that He would continue to do His work, for His glory. When I do this, it is surprising how often I hear positive reports some time later. I have had several seemingly failed healings, only to discover that healings manifested hours later, that night, or even as the patient woke up the next day. Sometimes people report feeling a hand touch them, experiencing warmth in the problem area, or something similar—and then they recognize that they have been healed. I can't explain why this happens, but I can say that I have seen it. And Jesus did say that those who believe would lay hands on the sick and *they would recover*—not necessarily that all would be immediately healed (Mark 16:18).

A fellow missionary was experiencing debilitating back pain. In fact, she was forced to postpone her return to the mission field as a result of the problems. Finally, through chiropractic care, she managed to make the trip, but shortly after her arrival in Africa, the pain returned and rendered her unable to do her work. I connected with her online and prayed for her back; she was immediately healed. The next day I inquired if the healing was sustained and she reported she only had pain in her tail bone. I prayed again and it was, again, completely healed. I then explained to her that she had to train herself to rebuke the condition if it crept back. She reported some time later that when the pain returned she was able to heal it herself through rebuking it and commanding it to go away.

Sometimes after our prayers and the manifestation of healing, sicknesses or pain *do* return. It takes faith to heal; it also takes faith to sustain the healing. For example, if someone's sprained ankle is healed by *your* faith, the next day that person is alone without you. If they feel just a little soreness, they may push it and push it, then convince themselves it was not healed. If they believe, on the other hand, they can simply rebuke the pain and command it to go away in Jesus' name; it will subside.

There have been times that this happened, and the person returned to me a second time for prayer. Upon their "re-healing," which confirmed the original work of God, they now had their faith boosted and confirmed the sufficiency of prayer to heal. When this happens, it is a good time to coach them to maintain the healing through their own faith.

What about anointing with oil during healing prayer? Personally, I don't always use oil—although there is biblical precedent for such practice. As with choosing a particular prayer style, if it increases your faith, by all means, do it. And if you also feel comfortable waiting for the elders of the church to pray, so be it. However, I believe that the passage in James which refers to these practices were written at a time when mature brethren would have been experienced in healing. Yet I would say that there is an overall lack of such experience today. Anyone who has faith to heal should be encouraged to pray for those who have needs.

When I went to Canada to visit my sick father, I went with an eager expectation for his complete and total healing from emphysema. My entire family had been praying for this opportunity for months. After our time visiting, I asked if we could pray for him and he seemed happy for me to do so.

"Emphysema go, now! Be healed. I command you to go in the name of Jesus Christ!" Nothing. Again I prayed. Nothing happened. One last time I prayed: firmer, more authoritatively, fervently. Nothing happened, again. I ended by asking God to do what remained to be done. It was in His hands, and on His timetable. I had failed. Not just then and there, but even in the weeks to follow, he exhibited no improvement whatsoever.

While visiting my Dad, we stayed with family and visited with a few of my relatives. For the most part, they are all cessationist Baptists, so things like healing and casting out demons are quite foreign to them. As we talked, some gave credence to what I was saying. Yet when it came time for me to demonstrate the power of prayer in Jesus' name, not one of them was healed. Carpal tunnel: nothing. Tinnitus: nothing. We saw no healings whatsoever among my family members. After hearing all the stories and examples from Africa, and then seeing none of it for real, I figured that they must think I had gone mad, or that I was simply making it all up.

When we visited my father the next day, he expressed some offense in my prayers of the previous day. He was embarrassed, hoping his neighbors had not heard. Weeks later I learned that his pastor brother had convinced him that I was simply mistaken, that these gifts were just for the apostles and ended with their deaths. As reported when Jesus visited His people in His hometown: "He could do no miracle there except that He laid His hands on a few sick people and healed them. And He wondered at their unbelief" (Mark 6:5-6). To my utter disappointment, I accomplished even less than that. And this would not be my last disappointment, either. In war time, not every battle brings a victory. You win some, and you lose some. But overall, our goal is to strengthen our position and keep advancing as much as possible against the enemy.

In the case of my family, I think perhaps they added "negative faith" to the equation and drained my faith reservoir for the healings. Another example was when my daughter, Rebekah, was suffering from a severely painful eye problem. We prayed several times and failed to see any improvement. I was discouraged. Then I coached her to believe, not just in Jesus to heal, but that she was indeed *already healed*, even though she did not see it yet (Hebrews 11:1, Romans 8:25). After praying again, I looked at her face intently for a moment and then confirmed that the pain was gone. I would not necessarily do this in all cases, but my daughter was of an age to begin to exercise her own faith and I knew that she did believe that healing was possible, so in this case what we did was effective.

Similarly, when people come to me for healing prayer here in Africa, yet really want medication or financial assistance to go to the hospital, prayers often fail. Those who clearly lack faith to be healed may pre-program the healer for failure. When I discern that medical treatment is a person's true intent, I often just send them to the clinic. If they recover and get the help they needed, praise God. God is still glorified, for even giving a cup of water in Jesus' name glorifies Him.

We will discuss in the next couple of chapters that a lot of sicknesses are the result of unclean spirits. If that is the case, and deliverance comes through prayer, then healing follows. Yet deliverance requires cooperation. If the demonized person welcomes and nurtures the unclean spirit, it will not be expelled by external force—at least, not permanently. This may explain why some sicknesses or injuries return after being healed through prayer.

Before we leave the subject of healing, I think it's important to consider "fake" healers, since many have refused to acknowledge the work of God because of these bad examples. Though it's easy to point fingers and it's a real temptation to dismiss this type of person, I think when we do so, it becomes just one more tactic of the enemy to completely discredit the power and manifestations of the Holy Spirit.

The Scriptures do command us to test the spirits, to confirm what is from God and what is not. Yet Jesus also rebuked the rulers of His day severely, even proclaiming their sin as unpardonable, for attributing the work of the Holy Spirit to an evil spirit. So how do we reconcile these two extremes?

First, the apostle John tells us in his letters what an antichrist spirit looks like: he will deny that Jesus is the Son of God, the Christ from God having come in the flesh. What does a false prophet look like? You will know them by their fruit: are their lifestyle and behaviors in accordance with what Christ taught, or otherwise? Even if someone appears like an angel of light, if they live contrary to Christ, do not follow them or their teachings. Their actions, not their words, accurately demonstrate their beliefs.

For example, look at the prophet of Islam. Did he deny that Christ is the Son of God, the Christ from God having come in the flesh? Also, did he live in accordance to the teachings of Christ, such as loving his enemies, not storing up treasures on earth, and so on? Regardless of his proclamation of having been a prophet of God (an angel of light), the conclusions are obvious. But the prophet of Islam was not a miracle-worker. What about them? Jesus answered this question directly:

John said to Him, "Teacher, we saw someone casting out demons in Your name, and we tried to prevent him because he was not following us." But Jesus said, "Do not hinder him, for there is no one who will perform a miracle in My name, and be able soon afterward to speak evil of Me. For he who is not against us is for us" (Mark 9:38-40).

Jesus said that if anyone is doing wonders in His name, do not hinder him, for he is not against us, but rather for us. Therefore, the litmus test of a false healer or deliverer is whether or not he is doing it in the name of Jesus. Does that mean the person is a straight teacher with honest motives? Absolutely not! Will they be perfect in everything? No. Even Paul said some preach Christ out of love and others because of selfish ambition; either way, we rejoice that Christ is proclaimed. We can test people's teachings by looking at the Word of God; if people are not living according to the truth, we should simply choose not to abide in their teachings.[xxi] Yet this does not mean that they lack faith or cannot operate in healing simply through the power and authority of the name of Jesus.

Someone healing by the authority of the name of Jesus is *not* an antichrist spirit; he certainly confesses Christ, which John claimed as the true test. Yet, based on the test of his "fruit," we may conclude that he is an unproductive saint. And we know what Jesus says will happen to branches that do not bear fruit: they will be cut off and thrown into the fire. Can a fruitless saint and a false teacher legitimately heal or expel demons in the name of Christ? Absolutely! Yet it will offer them little benefit eternally if they do not repent:

> "Not everyone who says to Me, 'Lord, Lord,' will enter the kingdom of heaven, but he who does the will of My Father who is in heaven will enter. Many will say to Me on that day, 'Lord, Lord, did we not prophesy in Your name, and in Your name cast out demons, and in Your name perform many miracles?' And then I will declare to them, 'I never knew you; depart FROM ME, YOU WHO PRACTICE LAWLESSNESS.'" (Matthew 7:21-23)

It is incumbent upon us to be careful about calling someone who heals and does miracles a fake, just because they have a questionable lifestyle or teach a compromised message. Christ's name is authoritative and powerful, independent of those factors. Call healings fake if they are indeed fake, such as if they are staged or the evidence is falsified. Do not attribute the works of God to Satan. Satan will not, I repeat *will not*, perform wonders in the name of Jesus. He fears and reviles that name. Even the early church warned against attributing the works of God to Satan.[xxii]

Ultimately, healing by the authority of Jesus is done to bring Him glory and to advance the kingdom of God, since Satan seeks to use anything and everything (including sickness and pain) to hold people in bondage. Let us rejoice in the work that is done in His name to bring freedom to those who most need it and certainly avoid discouraging such works. Let each one of us seek to participate in this life-giving work according to our faith, and engage in the battle that is before us!

Chapter 7—Direct Warfare: Expelling Demons

Malaria. Just malaria. *We can do this,* I thought to myself. I was walking with our mission's strongest front-line warriors. The blind see, the mute speak, the lame walk. What is malaria to God?

We were visiting a small village on the shores of Lake Victoria in Eastern Uganda. This was a return trip for me, and I had brought our guys with me to pray for three tough cases in particular. Yet I was amazed to discover that several people I had prayed for previously who had not been immediately healed were showing definite improvement. The most exciting news was that the mute boy who had not responded to prayer was now speaking!

I intended to pray for a boy with a swollen leg, but his father greeted us with the report that the boy's mother was in bed, severely ill with malaria. We immediately offered to pray for her, confident of God's ability to heal her. Entering the small mud hut, I rolled back the mosquito net to see a woman, not of sound mind, sweating yet shivering, all wrapped in covers. *Oh dear,* I thought nervously, *this is a serious case.* I gently touched her on the shoulder and commanded the malaria to go in the name of Jesus. Rather unexpectedly, the quiet atmosphere was instantly shattered. She began violently shaking her head back and forth, and I jumped into battle mode. A demon! I commanded the unclean spirit to go. The next several moments felt like the longest minutes of my life, as I saw no response whatsoever. The brothers behind me continued to support me in prayer, but my attention remained fixed on the writhing woman. Once again, I authoritatively told the spirit to leave. After what seemed like an eternity, the woman calmed. However, upon questioning, she indicated that she could still sense a presence. I continued to pray until she proclaimed freedom. As I then prayed for healing of specific symptoms, she rapidly regained strength and was able to sit up and speak. Her color returned and her fever abated. However, she still felt something in her chest. One more round of prayers and she was completely free, asking for food and drink for the first time in days.

This was not my first experience expelling demons, nor would it be my last. Though coupled with healing as a sign that Jesus said would accompany those who believe (Mark 16:17-18), I never considered that demons might be particularly prevalent or that this type of spiritual warfare would be common. Yet now I felt as if we had opened "Pandora's box." We were consistently encountering more and more demons as we performed healings and shared the gospel of the kingdom.

It is clear in the Scriptures that expelling demons was a routine part of the ministry of Jesus and the early disciples. The history of the first few hundred years of the church also reveals that this was part of normal Christianity.[xxiii] In fact, writings indicate that exorcisms were practiced by average, everyday believers.[xxiv] So what happened to all those demons, and why do Christians rarely see them today?

Since my goal is to mobilize the saints for spiritual battle, I believe that the practical is much more useful than the theoretical. However, some background may be helpful as you step out to engage on the front lines, particularly with such an obscure subject.

The early church believed that demons were the spirits of the Nephilim; that is, the mixed offspring of the angels that took human wives.[xxv,xxvi] There is some suggestion of this in Genesis 6:1-4, but it is also documented in the Book of Enoch, a writing widely accepted by the early church that is actually quoted by Jude in the New Testament (Jude 1:14-15). The Book of Enoch tells us that the rebellious angels were banished from Heaven while the immortal spirits of their mortal children were condemned to roam the earth until the final judgment. These bodiless spirits, which we call demons, are now basically parasites looking for hosts.

Whether you believe this particular account or not matters little. However, it is impossible to do the works that Jesus commanded and expected of us if we aren't willing to acknowledge the reality of demons and recognize their work. Regardless of where they come from or what we may call them, they are real. They are the enemy against whom we are called to fight.

The Scriptures identify Satan as a tempter, liar, adversary, and accuser. He is described as a lion seeking to devour (1 Peter 5:8). Both the fallen angels and the demons have, throughout human history, been understood to fight on the side of Satan in the cosmic battle that has continually been waged against God and His allies. The primary work of demons seems to be to afflict people with sickness, disease, suffering, and mental illness. When Jesus cast out demons, it was most often in association with some type of sickness or disorder (for example, Matthew 17:14-18, Mark 5:1-15), and when the demon left, healing was the result. That is why there is often a direct link between sickness and demons, though not all such afflictions are demons.

While in the US for several weeks (my first visit in over five years), I had the opportunity to talk to a middle-aged, Christian homeschool Mom. She poured out her heart about the difficulties in her home. Her husband had discontinued his medications for a psychological condition, bringing much conflict and instability into the home. Though I never welcome this situation (that is, lending an ear for a wife to vent about her husband), I quickly honed in on the underlying problems.

I shared my discernment with her: "You know these problems are spiritual?"

She agreed. I told her I thought there was something in her and asked if I could pray for her. With her consent, I commanded the unclean spirit to come out of her. Suddenly her face wore a cold, blank look. I saw the spirit of death, something darker and stronger than I had originally thought. I asked her if she had suicidal thoughts. She bowed her head and tears welled up. She had. I asked if it was in her family, and she responded with surprise that two of her children had challenges with suicide. I shared with her my discernment that her husband was suicidal, too.

I told her that her husband was not the enemy. Satan was trying to destroy her family. I counseled her that her family obviously posed a risk to the kingdom of darkness, or else the enemy would not be going to such great pains to keep them in bondage. I encouraged her to renounce the spirits of death and suicide and commanded the spirits to go in the name of Jesus. She felt immediate freedom, so I simply prayed for her to have the mind and peace of Christ, and for the Holy Spirit to come upon her. Immediately, she burst into a big smile.

I coached her to fight, fight, and fight some more in prayer. I told her to expect that Satan would not relent. This breakthrough she was experiencing would not come without a serious and swift counterattack. If she wanted to win the battle, she must love and support her husband. Her greatest weapon was prayer, that her husband's eyes would be opened to the realities of his bondage. Unclean spirits will not permanently leave those unwilling to renounce them. So she must pray for him to see these things and want change. Then Jesus could deliver him, and the whole family.

Upon our return to a larger group that was gathered downstairs, a friend of the woman commented, "Helen, you are smiling. I have never seen you smile before!"

I responded on her behalf, "Something just came out of her. She is free now."

The woman had a bewildered look. "Demons, in Christians?"

Though most people of my acquaintance in Africa are very open to the idea of demons (perhaps because of the prevalence of witchcraft, ancestor worship, and so on), this reaction on the part of Westerners to such activity is not uncommon. Yet the influence of unclean spirits on believers and non-believers alike is not limited by geographic location. Instead, I believe that Satan's tactic is to render Westerners oblivious to the presence of such spiritual forces of evil; we simply name and medicate them or write them off as unchangeable aspects of the sinful nature. One thing is for certain: as long as the demons know that you do not know that they are there, they remain a secret.

Before moving to Kenya, I can't say that I had ever considered the reality of unclean spirits around me in America. So of course, I saw very little of what I would now acknowledge as demonic activity— beyond, of course, identifying some of life's struggles, including sicknesses and such, as "spiritual warfare." Yet in my short three weeks visiting America, no less than a dozen people (the majority of them Christians) were delivered from the influence of unclean spirits. If only people knew, they could experience real freedom. Christ was sent to destroy the works of the enemy (1 John 3:8) and set the captives free (Luke 4:18-19).

Perhaps you would acknowledge demonic activity, but are like that incredulous woman in my story: "Demons, in Christians?" Think again about Satan's two wartime objectives: to keep people from proclaiming allegiance to Christ, and then, to render them inconsequential in the fight against God's greatest enemy. Christians are actually a *more* strategic target for demons than nonbelievers. A nonbeliever represents just one soldier gained or lost. However, a saint can do much damage to the kingdom of darkness if mobilized for battle (i.e., evangelizing, teaching, healing, exorcisms, and serving according to the leading of the Holy Spirit). The demons have huge incentive to attack the saints. The early church recognized demons as a threat to Christians and were vigilant in prayer against their influence:

> Moreover, it is also manifest to all, that we who believe in Him pray to be kept by Him from strange, i.e., from wicked and deceitful, spirits... For we do continually beseech God by Jesus Christ to preserve us from the demons which are hostile to the worship of God, and whom we of old time served, in order that, after our conversion by Him to God, we may be blameless. (Justin Martyr, *ANF* v. 1, 209. c. 160 AD)

One hang-up seems to be the idea of being demon "possessed." After all, demons can't inhabit the temple of the Holy Spirit, right? However, the term *demon-possessed* in the Bible is just the verb form of the word "demon" and is better rendered *demonized*. This does not have the same connotation as our English word, but rather has a range of meanings from being vexed or disturbed to being entirely under the complete control of a demon. So let us be careful not to use the English word "possessed" too restrictively, when uncertain if the demon is disturbing from the outside (vexed or disturbed by), or is present and in control from the inside. The early church understood this distinction.[xxvii]

Another consideration when it comes to unclean spirits is whether they are *impersonal* or *personal* spirits. Jesus' ministry documented almost exclusively personal spirits. Personal spirits are sometimes indwelling and sometimes externally influencing, bodiless spirits. Impersonal spirits are more like controlling behaviors, such as anger, bitterness, etc. New Testament authors discuss our ongoing battle with the *flesh*, which could also be understood as *impersonal* spirits of various kinds.

When it comes to the influence of demons upon Christians, I would speculate that most activity of personal spirits is external (in the form of outward disturbances) rather than indwelling in nature. Impersonal spirits (particularly, character issues that seem entrenched or strongholds that can't be overcome) are also common. I would not discount that a Christian could actually be indwelled by a demon, but that would only be if the steps of repentance, deliverance, and water baptism had not already occurred.

The early church believed that the Holy Spirit was present in a believer in measure, and would make Himself scarce (and even depart) if an unclean spirit were invited into the person. An example of this was already referenced in a previous chapter with the quote from the *Shepherd of Hermas*. What were there described as "evil spirits," including bitterness and anger, could refer to an actual indwelling demon. Yet the possibility remains that they were just impersonal spirits, with fleshly lusts being the underlying driver.

However, another example from the early church clearly demonstrates that a Christian was possessed by a personal spirit, or an indwelling demon:

> Why may not those who go into the temptations of the show become accessible also to evil spirits? We have the case of the woman—the Lord Himself is witness—who went to the theatre, and came back possessed. In the expulsion, accordingly, when the unclean creature was chastised with having dared to attack a believer, he firmly replied, "And in truth I did it most righteously, for I found her in my domain." Another case, too, is well known, in which a woman had been hearing a play actor, and on the very night she saw in her sleep a linen cloth—the actor's name being mentioned at the same time with strong disapproval—and five days after that woman was no more. How many other undoubted proofs we have had in the case of persons who, by keeping company with the devil in the shows, have fallen from the Lord! For no one can serve two masters. What fellowship has light with darkness, life with death? (Tertullian, *ANF* v. 3, 90. c. 197 AD)

In this case, the demon was not supposed to be there. And in no way am I implying that demon possession *should* be normal among

Christians. However, this demon clearly was welcomed and was therefore authorized, based solely on the Christian's attendance at a questionable venue (at that time, the theatre was considered secular and sinful). An alert Christian, one who is in the fight, will not be subject to such spirits. [xxviii]

I have seen unclean spirits, both personal and impersonal, influencing Christians, and even full demon-possession. They are invited when Satan is permitted to work in any of the three key areas of bondage we've already talked about: sin, strongholds, or victimization leading to anger, bitterness, etc. I will admit that in some instances it is disputable whether all the people in question were authentic Christians—that is, fully surrendered and baptized with genuine repentance—or whether they were faking or confused. Either way, it is incumbent upon us not to rule out the possibility of Christian demon possession because of some measure of uncertainty. If we misdiagnose the problem, we will be severely limited in dealing with it, because we will neglect to apply the appropriate tools. In that case, our enemy will have a sure advantage.

Thomas was a strong man, a confident man, yes—some would even say a prideful man. As a former football coach and karate instructor, he was a formidable presence in any room. However, this was not the Thomas I suddenly saw in front of me. This was a broken man. A man who had seen God, and seen himself in stark contrast. He had finally decided to surrender, and completely.

He boldly confessed before his fellow church *wazee* (elders) the many heinous acts he had committed—yes, even after his conversion. He was unfaithful to his wife. He stole money, and more. Everyone in the room sat quietly, in shock. They were not so much surprised that an African brother had done these things. But rather, they were amazed that he would voluntarily confess in such a public setting. In a culture where people say what you want to hear and try to minimize anything shameful, this was absolutely unheard of. But here he was, doing the impossible.

Following this meeting, I was already scheduled to meet with Thomas and pastor John, so that Thomas could be baptized in the Holy Spirit. My son, Isaiah, also joined us. I was actually quite relieved that Thomas had repented so deeply and openly. He had confessed to me just the week before that he suspected that he was being disturbed by an unclean spirit and had started fasting. I knew that if he was going to experience freedom, he needed to fully repent and renounce the strongholds he was now freely confessing.

We again began with songs and praise. John led this meeting in Swahili, so I honestly can't tell you everything that transpired. But I do know that when we began praying, a demon wasted no time in manifesting. As John, Isaiah, and I stepped in with a focused command for the demon to depart, Thomas went down, contorting his body and foaming at the mouth. We prayed until he grew calm and mentally responsive. Then I asked him if he was free. He said he was still very weak and he felt something in his throat choking him. We resumed prayer and he coughed it out. He jumped up, arms outstretched, and declared with a huge smile, "I am free, free, finally I am free!"

This was my first experience dealing with an obviously manifesting demon, the classical concept of what you would expect. As my Kenyan friends might say, I was not surprised...but I was surprised. I knew that Thomas had his struggles, but I also knew he was a sincere brother. How could he have a demon? At first these experiences led to more questions than answers.

In the field, I have encountered unclean spirits in several forms, typically during praise and worship or times of prayer (both of which unclean spirits resist). The most obvious is when the demons actually speak—a woman suddenly talking with a man's voice, for example, or a person yelling at you to leave them alone, even though they have invited you to pray for them—these are signs that a demon is manifesting. Odd or inappropriate behavior is also a clue. When someone starts flailing violently or screaming during prayer, you have got yourself a demon. Loss of physical control, such as weakness or even loss of consciousness, is likewise an unclean spirit. If you're paying close enough attention, you may see subtle changes in the eyes or countenance, such as a shift to blankness or fierceness. When I'm praying for the healing of pain in a specific area of the body and the pain suddenly migrates from one location to another, I immediately suspect a demon. No matter what form the manifestation of demons takes on, the next steps are the same: rebuke, command, and bind them in the name of Jesus, forcefully and authoritatively. They fear the name, so you don't need to fear them.[xxix] If you are inexperienced, it may take longer for the demons to actually leave, but if you persist with confidence, you should expect to see results.

Recall the dream I had of being escorted by an angel in the heavenlies and Satan approaching me? I was not fearful of him (though I was anxious a bit) because I knew he did not actually see me. He only suspected and sensed my presence. If, however, he had yelled in my face, "Human, go now! Marc, I command you, leave!" I would have freaked out. Well, that is what I imagine it feels like for these spirits. They are there but they know you don't see them, so they feel pretty comfortable. But once you start doing this work, you will likely find that they manifest quicker, and respond to your command more promptly. Perhaps they have heard from their roaming spirit friends how they had been exposed and expelled. And when you command, "Spirit of [fill in the blank], go now, in Jesus' name!" I suspect that they may sometimes believe you actually see them. You are right there in their face yelling at them—just imagine their fear.

If someone loses consciousness or falls down while you are praying for them, assume it is the result of unclean spirits. Personally, I do not believe in being "slain in the Spirit," which is what it is commonly called when someone reacts in this way, typically during prayer or the laying on of hands. In all my experience, every time someone has gone down, it was accompanied by the expulsion of an unclean spirit. Perhaps more significantly, there is no biblical or historical precedent for the Holy Spirit coming or filling a person and them going unconscious. It is always accompanied with lively gifts, such as tongues or prophesying. The only example I find in the Bible of someone going down as dead is when Jesus expelled an unclean spirit. I feel that this is important to share because it is potentially one more area in which Satan brings deceit in order to confuse the gifts of the Spirit and render them inconsequential. If you begin praying for someone and then think the Holy Spirit is manifesting and yet, the unclean spirit remains, you will be quick to proclaim victory when the victory really belongs to the enemy.

Another trick you might encounter is that demons have a tendency to "play dead" to get you to believe that they have gone. Don't fall for it. When a demon is expelled, there will be obvious changes: the host will regain strength and a smile, look of joy, or the feeling of freedom should be obvious. If you are still seeing a weak or sickly person, or if there are still oppressive feelings, ask if they are free or if they sense a presence. You may need to re-group and continue in prayer. If you have been working through repentance or strongholds with the candidate, you may want to ask deeper questions and try to discern if there is a root cause for the demon to be hanging on.

As you might have noted in Thomas' example, demons are often expelled by breathing or coughing out, just as the Holy Spirit comes by breathing in.[xxx] The word for "spirit" is akin to *wind* or *breath*, so it often helps to encourage people to cough or exhale when you are praying. Once I encountered a very stubborn demon, which would not go out until the person's mouth was opened and they actually vomited it out. I can't explain it, but somehow there is a link between the physical and the spiritual when it comes to expulsion.

I saw this in one particular example, where a young boy suffered from chronic respiratory issues and literally felt like a weight was removed from his chest upon prayer. The boy came to the gate of our Uganda home, complaining of a very heavy chest with persistent difficulty breathing. He said that especially at night, it felt like he had

100 kilograms sitting on his chest. I put my hands on his chest and commanded the sickness to immediately leave him. He exclaimed, "It's gone, it's gone!" He said it felt like a bird flew from his chest and he no longer felt the oppressive heaviness.

The next day he returned with his grandfather, reporting that he had slept perfectly for the first time in many years. His grandfather thanked me for his healing. I was sure that he had been delivered from an unclean spirit.

Though I've talked about some of the obvious signs of demons, as well as sharing some rather dramatic stories of their expulsion, this account illustrates that not all demons come (or go) with great fanfare. Many go out with an exhale or with tears. Those don't make great stories, but I don't want you to go away thinking that all exorcisms are spectacular, made-for-the-big-screen events. Many will depart effortlessly at the command in the name of Jesus.

Other situations are more dramatic and more difficult, of course. Some of our gifted brothers, along with a newly-baptized *Mzee*, were praying for a young boy during an all-night prayer meeting. And then the unexpected—the room lit up bright like the sun! What witnesses describe as a bolt of lightning came from the boy's torso and blasted the two experienced men back, leaving only the terrified new believer alone with the boy. Yet the boy was freed; the demon was gone.

No matter how they manifest, or how stubborn they are, you need not fear demons. They may try to scare you, or you may be startled by certain manifestations, but remember that Jesus has granted you all authority over the power of the enemy. The spirits are subject to you, and nothing will injure you (Luke 10:19-20). So proceed with great confidence to cast out demons in Jesus' name if you see or suspect their presence.

The boy could not speak. He had many of the issues one would expect in one diagnosed with autism. But a demon? I didn't see it. He was loving, joyful, kind, gentle—those are all fruit of the Holy Spirit. I wasn't entirely sure how to proceed. People with special needs were created by God, and we can't always discern His purposes; do we want to rush to pray away things that are blessings in disguise? In this case, I simply declined to pray for the time being.

On our second day together, however, I saw a completely different side to the boy. He was being difficult with the other children, even violent. When his father finally was forced to intervene, he was angry and destructive. He did not break anything, but he motioned like he would, and it was obvious that he wanted to. That, I told his parents, was something for which we could pray.

I summoned the boy, with gentleness and a big smile. He was still perturbed, but responsive. I sat him down and held his hands. I smiled as I stared him in the eyes and gently rebuked and commanded the spirits of anger, frustration, and violence to leave him in the name of Jesus. My words were firm, yet my tone was kind, so as not to disturb the boy emotionally. And it happened! His face changed on a dime. I knew he was delivered. I prayed for the peace of Christ to come upon him, and he responded with a glowing, ear-to-ear smile. He wasn't healed from his autism, of course, but the undesirable behavior (and its underlying spirit) was cleansed, and peace restored to him and to his family.

The lesson here? Don't presume that any or every mental condition, sickness, or behavior is a demon. Approach the situation with an open mind but watch with discernment as you pray. Look for signs or manifestations and keep following the clues. Discern, listening to the Holy Spirit as you proceed. Don't make a fool of yourself or Christ in trying to expel something that is not there.

Another take-away here is to remember that there is a real person being prayed for. I have found that during full manifestation, people often black out or simply do not remember what happened. But don't play around; just get it done. Don't have conversations with the spirits or make a big show out of it. Learning afterward that they had an unclean spirit can be a traumatic and often embarrassing experience, especially if other people are present. Do your best to handle things efficiently, and as respectfully as possible.

I've mentioned binding the spirits; this is a practice that comes from Jesus' words: "Truly I say to you, whatever you bind on earth shall have been bound in heaven; and whatever you loose on earth shall have been loosed in heaven" (Matthew 18:18). He also describes binding the strong man in the context of casting out demons (Matthew 12:24-29). I've seen that both sicknesses and demons can return, or unclean spirits even relocate to another family member upon expulsion. It is my interpretation that to "bind" a spirit can keep this from happening. So along with commanding spirits to leave, I add (more or less, depending on the situation), "I bind you in the name of Jesus. Go, and don't come back. Leave this family alone, and leave this household alone!" We will discuss tearing down strongholds in detail in the next chapter, which will keep demons from returning if they have had an open invitation from their host.

For me, casting out demons was something new and I've learned a lot and grown in confidence as I've progressed. Everyone who steps out on the front lines against all the spiritual forces of evil is going to question the reality of demons and their competence to expel them. In the following story, you can see that Matthew was just one of these young brothers.

A neighbor had flagged down Matthew, requesting that he bring me to pray for a sick old man in their village. Matthew, confident in his new-found knowledge of praying in the power of the name of Jesus, told the man that the white missionary was not needed. He could do it.

The elderly man's mud hut was filled with numerous neighbors, who milled around as if mourning. Upon seeing the weak and emaciated condition of the patient, Matthew wanted nothing but to return and get "missionary Marc." However, the Holy Spirit gave him the confidence he needed to proceed.

As he began praying, the man suddenly and unexpectedly shouted, "Leave us alone. We were invited!" Matthew was terrified. He knew what was happening, but had never expelled a demon before. He was just recently Spirit-filled and had seen many miracles in the field with me, but now he was alone. His first reaction was to break away and come get me, but he knew he could not back down now. He could not show his fear.

Matthew commanded that the demon depart in the name of Jesus Christ. After brief spiritual combat, the old man visibly calmed and returned to his senses. Matthew confirmed that he was free from the unclean spirit. After his deliverance, Matthew prayed for his health, and the man was immediately, completely healed.

I later returned with Matthew following this incident and confirmed the details of their meeting, as well as praying for more members of the man's family and sharing the gospel with them. Matthew's work, even in his uncertainty, provided an open door for God's victory over their bondage to Satan and sin.

Satan will use doubt and fear to his advantage, so be prepared. Stand firm and continue the fight in prayer until you see breakthrough. Just as with healing, expect to see God work through your obedience and faith. Your faith reservoir will fill up as you experience success in Jesus' name. Join our Lord in the battle to set the captives free.

Chapter 8—Releasing the Prisoners: Tearing Down Strongholds

All I could think was, *really, right during fellowship?* Yup, right in front of all her relatives and children, Mama Isabelle was on the floor, growling like a rabid animal. The meeting had changed directions in a moment: from singing and praise to an exorcism, right in this poor woman's sitting room. I rebuked the unclean spirit, the brethren rallying behind me. We prayed and prayed, with no discernable change. My voice was growing hoarse, my energy fading, and I dripped with sweat in the confinement of the room on that hot Ugandan afternoon.

Though we were all praying, all eyes were on me, everyone assuming I was the one with experience in these sorts of things. But nothing had prepared me for this. Sure, I had read about it, and prayed for people to be set free from strongholds, but at this point had never witnessed a full-blown demonic manifestation in such a public setting.

After many minutes of praying, fear gripped me. What in the world would I do if this demon did not leave? I had told it repeatedly to leave in Jesus' name. That was the beginning and end of my game plan. Finally, at my point of exhaustion and piqued fears, the woman grew calm. I instinctively began to praise Jesus. I suspected we weren't done, but I welcomed the respite. I knew I needed another approach. Something was amiss. And I doubted that such a public forum was an ideal place for dealing with the situation.

We proceeded with our meeting. After our fellowship meal, through a translator, I asked Mama Isabelle if she was free. As I suspected, she replied that she was indeed *not* free. After everyone left, I asked her some questions about the unclean spirits. She confessed her family history with witchcraft and how following the death of her uncle (a witchdoctor), all the family spirits had been transferred to her in the hope that she would continue the practice. That clarified the reason for the resilience of the opposing forces. I asked her if she wanted those spirits gone. She heartily conceded. I told her to verbally say that she was now a follower of Christ and declare that the spirits were no longer welcome and must leave her. She did it. I repeated her conviction and declaration to the Father and asked for His support in what I was about to do. Without even raising my voice, I told those unclean spirits to go, *now*, and never return. With just a sigh, they left without the least bit of resistance. She was free! Following a brief moment of private rejoicing, I petitioned the

Father to send His promised gift, the baptism of the Holy Spirit, upon our dear Mama Isabelle, and without hesitation she was filled.

How was it that these particular demons were so tenacious, and how do such spirits maintain their hold over people? As we've already discussed, Satan binds us in three ways: sin, strongholds, and unforgiveness. When we break these three chains, we can be set free.

Remember, Jesus was sent as a ransom to set us free from Satan, sin and the world. We receive this free gift by faith through repentance and baptism. In baptism, we die with Christ and rise again to new life—a new life in the Spirit (Romans 6:3-11). Yet, even as Christians, we do not always find freedom from sin or from weaknesses of character. This is a very discouraging reality for most, yet one that is able to be overcome through the tearing down of strongholds.

Though I've used this term repeatedly, I have yet to really define it. The word only shows up once in the Bible (in the spiritual sense meant in this book), in 2 Corinthians 10:3-6. It is rendered *fortresses* in some translations.

In context, strongholds are defined as "speculations and every lofty thing raised up against the knowledge of God...every thought..." Or, in the KJV, "imaginations, and every high thing that exalteth itself against the knowledge of God...every thought..." A stronghold, then, is a lie about God's truth, or a tool of Satan designed to confuse us into disobedience. These strongholds are the object of our spiritual warfare.

Sometimes (as in the case of Mama Isabelle), spiritual strongholds are generational in nature—lies and deceit that have been believed in the past by others and handed down as truth. In other cases, there are lies we have believed about ourselves or about God's Word that have simply become part of our personality or belief system. In either case, such strongholds have to be demolished if we are going to experience permanent freedom.

Practically speaking, how are these strongholds torn down?

Look again at the example of Mama Isabelle: once she verbally renounced those spirits, she was immediately and effortlessly delivered. Likewise, as she was fully cleansed, the Holy Spirit was immediately welcomed. Certainly, most Westerners don't have such overt and obvious demonic strongholds as this one, but we have strongholds nonetheless.

Our strongholds may manifest because of victimizations and the resulting bondage of anger, bitterness, or unforgiveness, as illustrated in just one example here in Kenya. A 17 year-old girl had twice come to our mission office to request medical treatment for stomach problems, with no definitive diagnosis and with no lasting improvement. She was attending a local secondary school and boarding with a neighboring family. Her caretaker brought her to us for prayer, since medical treatment had proven ineffective.

Upon their arrival, I asked Isaiah to take the lead, since he had recently healed a stomach ailment and I knew he'd have faith for it. We went to the prayer house on our property, and almost as soon as we laid hands on her, she immediately went down. A demon! We attempted to expel it, but it did not relent. As we continued to pray, the Lord revealed the spirit: *bitterness*. It was something that I just knew through discernment, so I went with it. We took a break, allowing her to regain control of herself, and then asked a pointed question: had she been abused? She would not look up and remained quiet. Something was amiss, but she wouldn't offer any more information. We asked her to come back the next day, alone.

The next day she shared more openly. This time, Titus had joined Isaiah and me for the prayer effort, knowing that a demon was likely to manifest. The girl was encouraged to forgive those who had abused her so that she could be released from any spiritual influences and healed of her stomach problem. She offered a verbal and heart-felt expression of forgiveness and personally renounced the spirit of bitterness. We were moving in the right direction.

We sang a few songs and began to pray. When I uttered the words "spirit of bitterness," she became an entirely different person at that moment: violent and uncooperative, repeatedly trying to escape the room. We blocked the exit and just kept commanding the spirit to leave her in the name of Jesus. Finally, she went limp. In a short time, she was calm and able to speak.

I asked her if she was free. She would not answer, so I could only assume she was not. The demon had offered a respite only to try to fool us into believing that it had gone. I could see hardness in her eyes; it was not the girl who had walked in that day. We resumed praying and the chaos erupted yet again. Eventually, we persuaded her into a chair and I could see that her mouth was clenched, as if preventing the expulsion of the spirit. I commanded her to cough it out and she clenched her mouth all the more. Eventually I gently opened her mouth with my fingers, and to my surprise, she vomited. The spirit had come out, and she was delivered! From there, everything became quiet and we resumed normal conversation. She was once again the engaging young girl that I had first met.

I prayed for her to receive the peace of Christ. She was restored to joy. Her stomach pain was also completely gone. She would return days later to hear the message of the kingdom of God. She was set free from Satan, and put on the path to salvation.

As we've discussed, the last chain Satan uses to bind us is unforgiveness. The anger, bitterness, resentment, and other emotions that result from unforgiveness put us in powerful bondage—you can see in this example just how resilient such spirits can be. Yet Jesus said if we do not forgive others, we will not be forgiven. Unforgiveness rarely hurts the perpetrator of an offense, but instead keeps the victim in bondage. That is why we must release those who have victimized us or sinned against us. Otherwise, we remain in Satan's grip.

In order to achieve true forgiveness, we must recognize that those who have hurt us are not our enemies. Rather, they are equally victims of our real enemy, Satan. Jesus and Stephen (Acts 7:59-60) were able to pray for their murderers. They knew it was Satan who had deceived them into committing their crimes. In both cases, the perpetrators literally thought they were serving and defending God. (This is a great example of a religious spirit, which is a common stronghold.) They are now awaiting eternal judgment because of Satan's deception; this is why Jesus said to love our enemies and pray for those who mistreat us. They are simply victims of Satan's devices.

A group of brethren surrounded Luke during one of our all-night prayer meetings. Two of our older church members prayed with fervency, yet no signs of deliverance were evident. Finally, the din subsided. They celebrated their victory, but did not realize that it had not yet been secured. Two of the more experienced, but younger, brethren knew that after sustained prayer, demons often go quiet to make it look like they have departed. The battle must resume. They suspected he was not free. The young brothers questioned Luke and confirmed their suspicions. Quietly, yet authoritatively, they commanded the demon to go. Without fanfare or hesitation, Luke was delivered.

Luke had been baptized just months prior. How was it possible that he was influenced by a demon? Were his repentance and baptism valid? Over the course of the next couple days, his story emerged. Luke's tools for his work as a mechanic had been stolen a week earlier. He confessed to extreme anger and bitterness. He also said that his heart felt different, spiritually, ever since then. Ephesians 4:26-27 warns against giving the devil a foothold by "letting the sun go down on your anger," but that is just what Luke did. He had actually invited an unclean spirit into his life through unforgiveness, anger, and bitterness.

A demon will return to its former host if, as Jesus said, the house is swept clean but left unoccupied: "Then it goes and takes along with it seven other spirits more wicked than itself, and they go in and live there, and the last state of that man becomes worse than the first" (see Matthew 12:43-45). Luke had said he had received the baptism of the Holy Spirit, but admitted later it was not true. In Luke's case, he had also grieved the Spirit through sin, leaving a place for unclean spirits to work in him.

One thing is for certain: unclean spirits seek a foothold and will always test the defenses. Like a thief, if the door is locked, they will try the window. But if the occupant of the house is awake and armed, an attempted robbery is unlikely. A determined robber, however, will simply wait until you're asleep and alone, knowing your defenses are down.

To avoid a "break-in" by the spiritual forces of evil, don't remain alone. Walk with brethren, especially those who will pray for you and encourage you to stand firm in your defenses. In the same way, if you fellowship with the Lord in prayer, always remaining alert, the enemy will be more likely to flee, and you will be safe from his influence. Whenever someone is delivered, baptized, or filled with the Holy Spirit, strong brethren around them should be aware and prayerful and surround them in fellowship, so that there will be less likelihood of a successful counter-attack.

We've talked about repentance and baptism and the laying on of hands for candidates to receive the Holy Spirit, but we did not go in-depth on renouncing strongholds, since that required a bit more of a foundation. So where do we start?

The best way to start is with fasting and completing a spiritual inventory, written or verbal, as we described in the chapter on receiving the Holy Spirit. All sins must be confessed and repented, strongholds renounced, and areas of victimization released. Strongholds can be either generational or personal. Strongholds also include witchcraft and curses, although I probably see that type of thing more in Africa than would be evidenced in Western cultures. As discussed previously, declare allegiance to Christ and freedom from Satan, renounce his claim on your life, and command those spirits to go in Jesus' name.

We discussed personal spirits (demons) in the prior chapter. Here we will deal with many impersonal spirits. They are what the New Testament writers call the *flesh*. The *flesh* is best described as our earthly nature apart from our divine nature, which is therefore prone to sin. The manifestations of the flesh are itemized in Galatians 5:16-21. James says that such natural, earthly wisdom is demonic and accompanied by every evil thing (James 3:15-16). So even if impersonal spirits are not actual demon *possession*, they are certainly demonically-inspired. In Scripture the *flesh* is oddly personified as having lusts and desires of its own and is described as being actively in opposition to the Spirit (Galatians 5:17). It is clear that if we live according to the *flesh* and not the Spirit, the end is death and failure to inherit the kingdom of God (Romans 8:6, 13, and Galatians 5:21).

79

These impersonal spirits may or may not have an actual demon behind them. Either way, we can command the spirit of "fill in the blank" to go, for the same result: freedom.

When someone is bound in a problem, their struggles can come from several possible sources. One is that they might simply need to confess and repent of a specific sin. We can't blame the boogeyman for everything in our lives; we need to take responsibility for our personal sins. The second possibility is that there is a personal demon. We covered that already, as it needs only to be identified and expelled. The third is an impersonal spirit, or, the *flesh*. No demon here, but rather, unwanted behaviors, thoughts, dreams, or character. Treat it just like a demon to obtain freedom—renounce it and command it to go. But in this case, it is then important to renew the mind, which we will cover more later.

If the candidate is already a "Christian" but is not yet baptized in water (or the Holy Spirit), that should be a priority, but only upon repentance and deliverance. Jesus said to enter the kingdom of God we must be born of water and the Spirit, so do that work. If it is complete, the mind still may need to be renewed. Pray for renewal of the mind, the mind of Christ, and the filling of the Holy Spirit. We must walk according to the Spirit, not the flesh; reckon ourselves dead to sin and alive in Christ (Romans 6:11). Everything of the flesh must be repented of, renounced, and released, so that we can be filled once again and empowered by the Holy Spirit. This should result in a complete transformation.[xxxi] As a solider in this battle fighting on behalf of your brothers and sisters, it is your responsibility to navigate the waters, carefully discerning the underlying root of any visible challenges so that victory will be assured.

So what are some common strongholds? I will cover the obvious ones first, and then address the subtle, yet often more destructive ones. This list is certainly not exhaustive, but simply provides a spring-board for your prayerful consideration. Some examples will be explained in more detail as we progress.

- Addictions: substances, sexual, porn, food and drink, gambling
- Factions (divisiveness): politics, religious, patriotism, racism
- Entertainment: sports, movies, music, novels, television, games
- Character: pride, greed, lust, jealousy, anger, rebellion, sexual deviance
- Worldliness: materialism, possessions, wealth, greed, theft
- Religious: false religions, denominations, cults, non-biblical worldviews
- Occult practices: witchcraft, séances, mediums, astrology, Ouija

- Personal: fear, doubt, insecurity, depression, anxiety, shame, suicide (death)
- Vindictiveness: judging, condemning, slander, gossip, accusing, revenge

There are more, but we will stop there for now. In the interest of space, I will not cover them in great detail. I do, however, want to highlight a few of the most strategic strongholds leveraged by Satan in order to accomplish his objective of rendering us ineffective and unproductive for the kingdom. Since these are strongholds, they are often well-hidden, but we are admonished to "walk in the light." As we shed light on Satan's plans, we have more of a chance of attaining victory in the ongoing spiritual battle.

Two key strongholds are religious in nature. The first I will simply call *worldly wisdom*, which is most often evidenced in "higher criticism" and intellectualism. The deception behind this stronghold says, *I know better than Christ.* We may read that Jesus said "such-and-such," but instead of taking it at face value, our response is, *I interpret it a different way.* Or we say, "What this *really* means is [fill in the blank]." Yet James tells us that worldly wisdom is jealous and has selfish ambition, and is not from above, but is earthly, natural and demonic (see James 3:13-18).

Jesus said we would be judged by His very words (John 12:47-50) and would "fall" if we did not act upon His teachings (Matthew 7:24-27). He also said that if we love Him, we will obey His commands (John 14:15, as just one example). John said if we do not obey Jesus, we don't know Him (1 John 2:3-6). Yet, this religious spirit and its associated stronghold typically refute all these Scriptures with a single assertion, which Christians have largely accepted as the beginning and the end of the gospel: "Believe in Jesus, and you will go to Heaven." No repentance, no obedience, no holiness, no righteousness, and no fruit necessary. It is a lie, a speculation against the knowledge of God, and a very strategic stronghold designed to keep people from finding salvation. The Bible is very clear that we cannot truly believe in the person of Jesus and in His salvation, while wholesale disregarding much of what He actually said. This stronghold, like any other, must be renounced, rebuked, and commanded to depart, so that the mind can be freed and renewed in the true knowledge of Jesus Christ.

The second very strategic religious stronghold is cessationism, or the religious assertion that the gifts of the Spirit ended with the death of the apostles—or, perhaps, with the assembling of the canon of Scripture. (I mention this specifically out of the many religious strongholds only because it is so relevant to the topic of this book.) This particular lie introduced by Satan was specially designed to render the church powerless, ineffective, and inconsequential in the fight for the kingdom. I have already discussed some of the problems with this belief and the biblical evidence for its untruth. It is my hope that my personal testimony throughout this book and the cited early church witness will demonstrate that the gifts are certainly still active, and are for everyone. Yet people still believe the lie, largely because they fail to see the Holy Spirit's power in their own lives. As I said earlier, it is a self-perpetuating stronghold empowered by doubt: they do not believe because they do not see, and they do not see because they do not believe. You now know it is simply a lie, a speculation against the knowledge of God. It has been exposed. Renounce it, rebuke it, and command it to go away in order to free your mind. Read the Scriptures with a new mind and ask the Holy Spirit to enlighten you to the truth.

The power of these religious strongholds lies largely in the creation of what the Bible calls "factions" and "dissentions." Culturally, we might call it "group think." Satan can easily perpetuate any stronghold when we splinter ourselves into little groups that all hold to the same lie. Almost every denomination has its "distinctives" and will defend them against all opposition—yet if that is the case, there is a good chance that a religious stronghold is present. Can you see Satan's purpose in encouraging denominations? And you can likewise see why Paul said that no one who practices factionalism will inherit the kingdom of God (Galatians 5:19-21). No denomination has a monopoly on the truth. This process of using factions is powerful for accomplishing just about any plan of the devil and perpetuating all forms of strongholds, or lies against the knowledge of God—even in the church.

Another type of stronghold worthy of mentioning further is the "personal" strongholds listed above. They are often overlooked because they do not directly hurt others. The quiet housewives whom we presume are angels in disguise are often secretly enslaved to Satan via this type of stronghold. Fear, doubt, insecurity, anxiety, depression, and shame are very powerful for rendering a person inconsequential and ineffective for the kingdom of God. Sometimes they have childhood experiences or generational patterns at their root. Yet they are still lies that need to be exposed, bound, and sent packing. We need to confront these strongholds directly and forcefully to gain freedom. Once freedom is proclaimed, this type of stronghold needs to be kept from returning through an aggressive renewing of the mind and proclamation of God's Word.

Very often, these strongholds interact with one another in a very sinister way. As we live in relationship to one another (husband/wife, parents/children, or even brothers and sisters in Christ), we need to be aware of the spirits and how they may provoke one another. I think we would all acknowledge that those closest to us know best how to "push our buttons." This is actually a spiritual issue, and one that is quite hidden by our enemy. The spirit in the wife, for example, knows the spirit in the husband intimately. Imagine a woman who has a rebellious spirit. She is contentious, disrespectful, and difficult to please. Her husband has an angry spirit; he is easily provoked, often irritable, and harsh. These two spirits play off each other to keep up friction and strife in the marriage, which should be a "safe haven" for both if they are professing Christians.

How about a passive-aggressive spirit with a controlling spirit, or a husband who has a spirit of lust with a wife who has a spirit of shame? Most of us could probably look at some of the most significant relational conflicts in our life and, with the help of the Holy Spirit, see the underlying work of personal or impersonal spirits. This is an important element of a thorough "spiritual inventory," as we know that our enemy works through very insidious means.

Freedom from sin and freedom from strongholds are dealt with in slightly different ways, but both must be maintained through constant vigilance and resistance to all the enemy's work. When you have sin in the camp, it must be routed out: confessed, repented, and cleansed by the blood of Jesus, then continually resisted by the strength that God provides. However, we can't repent from a spirit, just the sin that empowers that spirit. Spiritual strongholds must be renounced and we must be delivered through prayer, then our mind renewed by God's Word and the Holy Spirit. If you give the enemy an invitation or opportunity to return, through active sin or simply spiritual laziness, rest assured, he will. Deliverance is not simply a one-time event, but takes ongoing vigilance, repeat meditation and review, resistance through prayer, accountability, and time in the Word. Resist the devil, and he will flee from you.

Chapter 9—He Sent Them Two by Two: The Battle Plan

A blind man healed—*no way!* Never would I have believed it had I not witnessed it.

It was a sunny afternoon in a coastal fishing village in Eastern Uganda. It was March of 2017, just months after God had taken over the East African mission with His presence and His power. I was traveling with Matthew, a young disciple who was recently Spirit-baptized, and who had already witnessed several miracles himself.

I have always been attracted to water. I love the ocean, lakes, ponds, and rivers. Fishing, boating, and swimming used to be my interests. At my age, now I just like sitting by the water and enjoying the sights and sounds while relaxing, praying, or reading. Yet it never escaped my notice that Jesus' public ministry started at the water with fishermen, or that Paul found Lydia at the river. Well, that was where we were going: villages on the shore of Lake Victoria, a 17-million-acre tropical lake.

When we arrived at the small village, we found a good place to park our motorbike and meandered along the shore, where eventually we happened upon a small group of people doing their chores on the lakeside some several hundred meters out. We greeted them and asked if they would permit us to share the gospel of the kingdom with them. About eight people gathered: some, fishermen tending to their nets; others, mamas doing their laundry; and a couple that were simply loitering by the water's edge. I began teaching them our introductory message—what we call *The Two Kingdoms*—just from memory, without tracts or a Bible. I wasn't there to win souls, but rather to find a man of peace: that person who would organize others for deeper teachings in their home at a follow-up visit. The small crowd was very receptive.

Following the teachings, I asked if anyone wanted prayers for healing. Two women responded. One had severe lower-back pain, and the other had problems with her leg. First I prayed for the leg problem, an ailment with which I had prior success. The look of shock on her face when she was healed was priceless. She would not stop pacing about, trying to re-create the problem, but it was gone. Next, the back problem: same result. Now I had everyone's attention. I reassured them that I was not a special person, but rather that the name in which I prayed, the *Jesus* of the message I had just shared— *He* was their healer.

Then one of the onlookers, a young man named Joseph, asked me to go to his family's home to visit some patients there. I agreed, but only after we scheduled a follow-up with the woman with the leg problem. She would host meetings for the next several weeks with her family, neighbors, and friends. She was our person of peace.

We were welcomed to the compound of Joseph's grandfather, approximately two kilometers from the shore. The host was blind—not entirely "lights out," but rather, groping for your hand to greet you and unable to see any faces. We would call his condition *legally blind*. Once inside the home, I shared a much-abbreviated message before being interrupted.

Apparently, the two women who had been healed had gone to market to proclaim that a *mzungu* [white person or European] was in the village healing people. Now, numerous people were crowding into the small mud hut. I asked them their problems, and methodically began praying—that is, commanding sicknesses to depart. The old blind man was first. But as it turned out, he had four problems, not just one: his foot, knee, back, and eyes. So I started where I had had prior success. The foot: healed. The knee: healed. The back: healed. Now everyone was amazed, including myself, and the faith in the room was over the top (mine, the old man's, and the onlookers'). We all added to the reservoir. I was actually thinking, *Wow, this could happen.*

I put my fingers on his eyes and commanded the spirit of blindness to go, and for healing and restoration to come. He opened his eyes and cupped my face with a huge grin, exclaiming, "I can see you!" He walked to each person in the room, saying the same thing. Amazed, I continued to pray for those who had gathered, at least eight in all. Everyone was healed except for one boy with elephantitis. Finally, Joseph himself, along with his grandparents, shared their conviction that he had a demon. They wanted to know if he could be delivered. I commanded the unclean spirit to go away. I saw nothing that led me to believe that he had been delivered, but he said he felt free.

Even after all this excitement, the visit was not over just yet. An elderly woman who had heard all the rumors at the market arrived, requesting that we visit her home to pray for a mute five-year-old boy and a mute and lame patient with HIV. We went and prayed but saw no improvement with either condition. We started for home with a feeling of failure. Yet before we could ride off on our motorbike, we were corralled into a lame woman's home. We prayed for her and she immediately walked! From there we departed, praising our God.

The next time we visited the village, I confirmed that the evil spirit had left Joseph permanently. I was surprised to find out that the boy with elephantitis, who had not been healed, was rejoicing because after prayer his leg had become pain-free, his flexibility had increased, and the tissue had softened. And to our amazement, the mute boy was speaking and the lame and mute HIV patient was speaking, eating, and able to stand. God had done amazing miracles in the lives of every patient, even though full healings had not been immediately evident.

You can see that as I approached a new place and new people with the intent to share the gospel, I found a group, asked their permission to teach, and then followed up with healing and the casting out of demons, works of God which gave validity to the message *and* revealed a "person of peace" with whom I would later follow up with further teachings. Evangelism was never meant to be confusing. Jesus specifically instructed His disciples how to do it. However, (for the most part) I do not see Christians following this pattern; perhaps people assume that these instructions were only for the twelve apostles and the seventy others he sent out. Yet because of the scope of the "Great Commission" (for all disciples *to the end of the* age), these instructions are just as valid for you and me as they were for Jesus' original audience.

Luke 10, where we find Jesus sending out His disciples, contains vital instructions for front-line kingdom expansion warriors. It is the essential battle plan for our attack on the kingdom of darkness. Let's look at the instructive passage for which the "Luke 10 evangelism" method is so aptly named, and then we'll discuss it a bit.

> Now after this the Lord appointed seventy others, and sent them in pairs ahead of Him to every city and place where He Himself was going to come. And He was saying to them, "The harvest is plentiful, but the laborers are few; therefore beseech the Lord of the harvest to send out laborers into His harvest. Go; behold, I send you out as lambs in the midst of wolves. Carry no money belt, no bag, no shoes; and greet no one on the way. Whatever house you enter, first say, 'Peace *be* to this house.' If a man of peace is there, your peace will rest on him; but if not, it will return to you. Stay in that house, eating and drinking what they give you; for the laborer is worthy of his wages. Do not keep moving from house to house. Whatever city you enter and they receive you, eat what is set before you; and heal those in it who are sick, and say to them, 'The Kingdom of God has come near to you.' But whatever city you enter and they do not receive you, go out into its streets and say, 'Even the dust of your city which clings to our feet we wipe off *in protest* against you; yet be sure of this, that the Kingdom of God has come near.' (Luke 10:1-11)

There is much that could be said about this whole passage, but some is self-evident, so we'll just jump to the highlights. First, note that these instructions were not just for the apostles. In Luke 9, Jesus had sent the twelve to do the same work, but here He extends the work to seventy others. Jesus further expanded this to *all* successive disciples of the apostles in all nations for all generations—yes, even you and me (Matthew 28:18-20).

The next point is that He sent them *out*. This is not church work, this is field work. The front-line battle is *out there*, plundering the kingdom of darkness. We are to be sheep bravely entering into the wolves' territory, not sheep inviting wolves in, hoping that something we say or do will eventually convert them. I truly believe that if Christians had continued to follow the method of evangelism given by Jesus, rather than abandoning it for their own ideas, the work of spreading the gospel would have already been completed and Jesus would have already returned.

Another important point: they were sent in pairs. I can think of several reasons for this practice. The first is accountability. Sending a minister alone can present him with various temptations. The second reason is security. Sheep *baa baa*-ing among the wolves is certain to pique the enemy's interest. When implementing Luke 10, there are challenges with objectors, authorities, travel difficulties, and anything else Satan can throw at you. Two people can more easily overcome such obstacles. A third reason for going in pairs is because two can run faster than one. Jog alone, and you are sightseeing—but run in pairs, and you have a race. With a ministry companion, I find myself much more emboldened to engage prospects and plunder the enemy camp, pressing forward even in the face of obstacles.

Finally, two-by-two field work is also the perfect opportunity for discipleship, since a seasoned evangelist can walk with a novice. A mentor will have plenty of opportunity to model the work, then the two can minister cooperatively, and at some point the young disciple can take the lead under the supervision of his mentor. Eventually he will be able to do the work himself as a fully equipped front-line soldier. He can then repeat the training process himself with a new disciple.

Jesus said, "The harvest is plentiful, but the laborers are few." Personally, for me, Jesus' words here really take the pressure off. It is comforting to realize that *the people God has prepared for the kingdom are ready to hear the message.* I need only to go out in obedience and follow the leading of the Holy Spirit. Some may complain that "the soil is too hard;" yet, our Lord and King explicitly said *it is harvest time.* We just need to pray that we can discern those whom God has prepared—seek them out, and engage them.

There are few more obvious examples of this cooperative work than one particular day when I was doing a pastoral training mission and we were in the two-by-two evangelism training phase. Two pastors and our field evangelist approached a home and were warmly welcomed by the Mama of the house. Three cups and a hot pot of chai were awaiting them at the table. She told them she was expecting them. The Lord had showed her in a dream the night before that three men of God would visit her that morning to teach her about the kingdom of God. The pastors were amazed that God had pre-organized their visit. As we go out, we must go in faith, believing that God has already prepared those who will receive.

The problem is not that there is no harvest, but that there is a serious labor shortage. The impetus of this book is to make more laborers—front-line soldiers for the kingdom of God. Pray for more, yes, and get out there and make more disciples yourself.

Even if the harvest is ready, don't for a second think that this work can be accomplished without cost or challenge. For Jesus also said, "Go; behold, I send you out as lambs in the midst of wolves." The message of the kingdom of God is a direct, frontal attack on the kingdom of darkness. The power of the prince of the air will not simply step aside while you aggressively attack his domain. Expect a counterattack, and resist him in prayer.

Jesus said, "Carry no money belt, no bag, no shoes..." (Luke 10:4). We can't engage in the mission with any worldly thing of perceived value, otherwise the prospect will seek the worldly benefit in lieu of the kingdom message. This is very important and has universal applications. Seeker-sensitive and benefit-based methods of attracting nonbelievers can help to draw a crowd, but will do little to get people interested in the authentic kingdom message. Jesus' message was one of self-sacrifice and commitment, counting the personal cost (as we will discuss in Luke 14:25-33 shortly). Jesus never used benefits to make disciples. Yes, He loved people and met them at their place of greatest need (specifically, in healing and casting out demons to bring freedom to the oppressed). But He never entertained them or dumbed down the message—the hard message of the kingdom of God.

Jesus said to look for the man of peace and stay with him, not moving from house to house (Luke 10:5-7). We are not instructed to engage numerous people with broadcast, shotgun-approach evangelism. Instead, we are praying and observing, listening to the Spirit to direct us in a more relational manner to this "man of peace." This process takes discernment.

Gifted evangelists may engage crowds, as Jesus, Paul, or Peter and John did when they taught in the synagogues and other quasi-public places. If Jesus meant for us to relationally look for a man of peace, what is the purpose for public evangelism, and does it present a contradiction in method? In Acts 17:1-10, Paul preached to the masses in a public setting; most rejected, but some received the message. They were chased to Berea and the process repeated. This time, Paul left strong teachers behind to strengthen the new disciples. We then read in Acts 20:4 that Paul was accompanied by disciples from both Thessalonica and Berea, and that his purpose was to continue their discipleship. We can infer that public evangelism is designed to identify men of peace, who we then engage in longer-term discipleship in a more personal setting, as Jesus talks about in Luke 10.

Jesus said *not* to go house-to-house. Couple this with not greeting anyone along the way, and we see that this directly conflicts with some modern, house-to-house evangelism techniques. While we may focus on winning converts and covet large numbers, Jesus was looking for a smaller number of committed disciples. His teachings certainly reveal that He was not looking to entice people to make a decision by emphasizing the benefits of joining His "movement:"

> Now large crowds were going along with Him; and He turned and said to them, "If anyone comes to Me, and does not hate his own father and mother and wife and children and brothers and sisters, yes, and even his own life, he cannot be My disciple. Whoever does not carry his own cross and come after Me cannot be My disciple. For which one of you, when he wants to build a tower, does not first sit down and calculate the cost to see if he has enough to complete it? Otherwise, when he has laid a foundation and is not able to finish, all who observe it begin to ridicule him, saying, 'This man began to build and was not able to finish.'... So then, none of you can be My disciple who does not give up all his own possessions." (Luke 14:25-33, portions)

Jesus used the crowd as a means of identifying people who were willing to count the cost, surrender everything, and follow Him unconditionally.

Thus, our man of peace is simply the person that the Spirit has already prepared, such that when we present the hard teachings, the high cost, and the total commitment necessary for becoming a kingdom disciple, they willingly surrender. So why *stay* with the man of peace, as opposed to praising God for the conversion, and moving on?

When the man of peace is identified, we preach the kingdom, bring him to complete surrender to Christ, take him through repentance, baptize him, see him filled with the Holy Spirit, and teach him to obey all that Christ commanded. This is a major time commitment. There is no quick decision and magic prayer, and then invite him to church. The harvest worker remains with the man of peace and slowly and methodically teaches him and his household.

Whether we are ministering to unchurched, cultural Christians, or Muslims, we can use the same method and the same message. During a pastoral training seminar, I once taught that there is no fear in teaching Muslims (especially in a free country). I explained that I had taught and baptized several Muslims. The organizing pastor wanted to see it with his own eyes, and more or less dared me to teach a Muslim when we went out for field evangelism. I asked him, "Do you know where any Muslims live?"

He replied, "No, but there's a mosque here."

Off we went to the mosque to find a Muslim. Well, we hit the jackpot: the Imam and his family lived next door. I asked if we were welcome to enter his home to teach him about the kingdom of God. I literally made him verbally ask me to teach it, because I refused to teach in his home without his consent. He said, "Yes."

I prayed a prayer of peace and taught our *Two Kingdoms* tract. He had some questions and I answered them one by one, never directly insulting Islam or Mohammed. In response to certain inquiries, I used Scriptures to make clear what I believed, or simply said, "You know what I believe about that, why must you hear me say it?"

When I was done teaching, I asked him if he had any needs that required prayer. He immediately responded that his daughter had been very sick for a long time and he had invested everything he had, but the medical establishment did not help her. I asked for her and he carried her to the room we were in. I laid hands on her and prayed for her healing in the name of Jesus. At that point, our meeting was over; we shook hands, and I went home.

I came to learn a year later that his daughter had been immediately, permanently, miraculously healed. The Imam surrendered his post in weeks and stopped attending mosque entirely within months. He read and re-read the *Two Kingdoms* tract I had left with him and was convinced that the One who had the power to heal his daughter must be the One True God. A year later, he found me through an incredible set of circumstances and he surrendered to Christ, repented, renounced Islam, and is a very strong, Spirit-filled brother hosting a home fellowship and leading others to Christ to this day. He was a man of peace.

You can see the important role that God's miraculous healing can play in people receiving the kingdom message. Jesus said to proclaim "the kingdom of God is here" when someone is healed, because sickness and demonic oppression are the work of the enemy. When people are delivered, we take ground for the kingdom of God. How do you suppose people would respond if you declared, "The kingdom of God is here!" but in the name of Jesus they were *not* healed? They would say that your kingdom looks a lot like theirs. We perform healings and deliverance in Jesus' name in order to demonstrate the superiority of God's kingdom as we share the message.

Some think that the gifts and works of the Spirit are a crutch, and that people will put faith in them while disregarding the Word of God.

This is not true. The Bible says we should expect to see these manifestations of the Spirit; therefore, they confirm the truth of the gospel. In fact, it is those who *lack* faith that do not see these manifestations, because they deny the reality of the truths written quite plainly in God's Word.

Jesus never told us to debate, argue, or convince people into the kingdom. He told us simply to proclaim the message—the positive message. I really wish I knew that when I was a young Christian. Being zealous and exuberant, and having studied not a little bit in apologetics, I rather enjoyed a good debate. Perhaps there is a place for that, but it is not part of Jesus' instructions for evangelism. If the prospect is good-hearted, they will be receptive to the truth.

In its final point, Luke 10 says that if a good-hearted man of peace does not welcome you, simply dust off your feet and move on. This requires just as much faith as any other step in the process. It can be hard to know when to persevere in looking for a man of peace and when to move on; discerning and trusting God's leading is essential.

In the beginning of this chapter, you saw the success of a "classic" Luke 10 mission on the shores of Lake Victoria. Yet this was not my first attempt there. I had visited a similar shore village, where they initially welcomed the teachings about the kingdom of God, but refused to bring any sick for healing. A second visit revealed that there were rumors circulating throughout the village that we were devil-worshippers, and so organizing anyone for future teachings proved difficult. They were also suspicious about prayers of healing, so there were no demonstrations of the power of Jesus' name. This is just one example where it seemed obvious that we needed to "dust off our feet" and move on.

Honestly, I don't like how Luke 10 is written. The entire purpose of the mission (preaching the kingdom, healing the sick, and expelling demons) seems to be obscured and almost inadvertently alluded to at the end. On the other hand, Luke 9, where Jesus instructed the twelve apostles alone, contains many of the same instructions but cuts right to the point of the mission at the very beginning.

In Luke 9:1-2, Jesus gave the disciples power and authority over all demons and to heal diseases. Then He sent them to preach the kingdom of God and to heal the sick. We see later in Luke 10 that they were told to heal the sick and that the demons were subject to them in His name. There is little doubt that the seventy received the same exact authority and instructions as the twelve, and applied those methods with the same results (see Luke 10:11, 17-20).

The gospel of the kingdom that Jesus tells us to share, the very theme of the Christian message, is in the Lord's Prayer: to establish His kingdom on Earth the way it is in Heaven. The three weapons in our arsenal (given by Jesus right here in Luke 9 and 10) are preaching that message, healing the sick, and expelling demons. It matters little which of the three you lead with, but you need to be armed with all three when you head out to battle.

The early church recognized that the power manifestations were given specifically for evangelism.[xxxii] However, if you lead with healing or deliverance, be sure to follow with the kingdom message. If you lead with the gospel, be sure to offer healing and deliverance. They are all for the benefit of the prospect, and all demonstrate the love and power of God for His ultimate glory. Just listen to the Holy Spirit as you go out. Do the work to its completion, just as Jesus instructed.

So what exactly *is* the gospel of the kingdom? If this is the message that we preach when evangelizing, healing, and delivering the lost, it's essential to be able to share it with clarity.

If you ask someone what Christianity is about, the stock answer will be something like, "God's redemptive plan for humanity." But Jesus only mentioned dying on the cross for our sins a handful of times. He talked about our need to be born again just once. He discussed being sent as a ransom once. He only mentioned church twice. Yet the "kingdom of God" is mentioned about 100 times in the New Testament. You'll notice that most of Jesus' parables start with, "The kingdom of God may be compared to...," and then He tells a story.

Jesus said He was sent to Earth to proclaim the kingdom of God (Luke 4:43). What Jesus sent His disciples to do was exactly what He had been doing (Luke 9:2, Mark 4:23, and Matthew 9:35). Jesus explicitly stated that the end of the world would not come *until the gospel of the kingdom* was preached to all nations (Matthew 24:14). That is exactly what His followers proceeded to do after His death and resurrection (Acts 8:12, 28:23, and 30-31). In fact, the establishment of this kingdom on Earth was what Jesus commanded His followers to pray for (Matthew 6:10, Luke 11:2), and the culmination of God's work is the fulfillment of this prayer (Revelation 11:15).

In my opinion, the best passage to summarize the gospel of the kingdom is Colossians 1:13-14: "For He rescued us from the domain of darkness, and transferred us to the kingdom of His beloved Son, in whom we have redemption, the forgiveness of sins." In essence, we all start off as enslaved to Satan under the law of sin and death (Romans 5:12). Jesus was sent as a ransom to redeem us from bondage (1 Timothy 2:5-6). Since Jesus never sinned, death was powerless over Him and He rose from the dead and conquered death (Acts 2:24). Through repentance and baptism, we can partake in His death and resurrection (Romans 6:2-7); by His shed innocent blood, our sins can be cleansed (1 John 1:9). Therefore, when we die according to the flesh, death will likewise have no power over us and we will resurrect at the last trumpet (1 Corinthians 15).

How do we enter the kingdom of God? Quite simply, through water baptism and receiving the Holy Spirit (John 3:5). It would also be accurate to say that the kingdom enters *us* (Luke 17:20-21). However, entrance is just the first step—only *inheritance* is permanent. The branches, though they have been grafted into the Vine, will not all remain, except if they bear fruit (John 15:1-10). In the same way, unrighteous saints will certainly not inherit the eternal kingdom, in spite of having entered through baptism and receiving the Holy Spirit (1 Corinthians 6:9-10, Ephesian 5:5-6, Galatians 5:19-21).

Depending on your Christian background, perhaps these teachings are as foreign to you as they were to me at the time I was first exposed to them. Yet this is exactly what our New Testament teaches, as validated by the early church. The thesis is this: Christ was sent to redeem us from the domain of darkness, cleanse us, change us, and impart the Holy Spirit in us, such that we can abide in His teachings and bear fruit unto salvation. We are saved by grace through faith. We offer faith; He returns His divine power (grace—see Titus 2:11-14) to change us. Why? So that we can walk in the works He prepared for us to do (Ephesians 2:10), and so that by persevering in righteousness and holiness we will receive the promise of eternal life. (Hebrews 6:4-6, Hebrews 10:26-31, 2 Peter 2:20-22).

This is the gospel of the kingdom preached by Jesus, the apostles, and the seventy. This was the gospel Philip brought to Samaria (Acts 8:12). This was the gospel that Jesus gave Paul on the road to Damascus (Acts 26:16-20). It was the very message Paul was teaching (Acts 28:23, 30-31). This is the revolutionary message that we need to understand to become effective in the front-line battle, because this is the message that must be preached as we go out as soldiers for the kingdom of God.

Jesus summed up all the commandments of God into two: love God and love others. This should undergird our fight for souls in the battle against the Prince of this world. God loved the world and sent Jesus to preach the kingdom, heal the sick, and expel demons. Now we are His hands and feet and are called to do the same. Rescuing people from the kingdom of darkness and transferring them to the kingdom of light is the good work of the good news. The playbook for victory is right here in Luke 10. Let's get back to basics, do what Jesus said, and mobilize fellow laborers who will get out there with us into the harvest field.

Chapter 10—Orders from the Top: Hearing from God

You may have noted in several of my testimonies that the gift of discernment played a large role in how I prayed for people or ministered healing and deliverance. Though discernment is a spiritual gift to be given how and when God desires, I do believe that he prepared me to receive it long before I came to Africa, through many of my experiences as a maturing Christian in America. It starts with learning to hear and respond to God's voice—a vital necessity for every Christian on the front lines of the battle, regardless of your gifting or calling.

"Buy what you need and I will pay for it."

That's what I heard. My minivan was getting old and getting small. That is, my family was growing yet again. Normally, buying a vehicle was not a big challenge. I always had good-paying jobs and excellent credit. But this was different. Just months earlier, the Lord had told me to leave my job to write a book. Without hesitation, I complied. I then cut up our credit cards. And I refused to tell people of our needs. I wanted us to trust in God, not in the good will of others, government assistance, or credit. Jesus said if we seek His kingdom and His righteousness, He would provide for our needs. I believed Him. Yes, the Bible says if you don't work, you don't eat. But I was working, doing what He told me to do. He would have to feed me like Elijah, and even pay my mortgage.

We had no savings and I was unemployed. How would I buy—not be given, but *buy*—a van? I wasn't sure about that, but I was sure about what I'd heard, so I went shopping. I saw an ad for a 15-passenger, off-lease church van with just 5,200 miles on it several hours from our Connecticut home. I called the seller and we agreed on a price. Then he asked what I knew was going to be the deal-breaker question: "How do you want to pay for this?"

I told him straight, "I don't have money. I don't have a job. I was just told by the Lord to get what I need and He will pay for it."

He asked me how I was surviving. I told him work would come to me: changing brakes, rebuilding a carburetor, a consulting job, selling items, and so on. He asked how much I made consulting. I told him, and he listed that as my income, and the loan was approved. He agreed to send the van, yet sight-unseen, to my home with the papers for me to sign the next day. Deal! I had a new van with no clue how I would be able to pay for it.

One hour later, I received a surprise phone call from a previous employer. Though I had left the company years earlier, I still held some stock that I had acquired through my employment. But now they informed me that the company had been purchased, and all stock-holders were being bought out. I could expect a check for an unexpectedly large sum of money in just two weeks. God paid for my new van and then some!

As a younger Christian, such as during the time illustrated in this story, I expected that if God Himself was going to say something to me, He would thunder from the clouds with the voice of James Earl Jones. You know, like He did for Jesus at His baptism or during the transfiguration. However, for me, it has never been like that. The Scriptures give a great illustration of how God speaks to His people in the example of Elijah:

> So He said, "Go forth and stand on the mountain before the Lord." And behold, the Lord was passing by! And a great and strong wind was rending the mountains and breaking in pieces the rocks before the Lord; but the Lord was not in the wind. And after the wind an earthquake, but the Lord was not in the earthquake. After the earthquake a fire, but the LORD was not in the fire; and after the fire a sound of a gentle blowing. When Elijah heard it, he wrapped his face in his mantle and went out and stood in the entrance of the cave. And behold, a voice came to him and said, "What are you doing here, Elijah?" (1 Kings 19:11-13)

God did not show Himself in the gale, the earthquake, or the fire. Rather, He was present in the gentle breeze. I believe that the reason for this quiet communication is that God is reaching out to those with faith, those who are seeking, and those who are attentive to His gentle call.

You will need to get used to the variety of means that He will use to communicate with you. I remember the time I was looking for a yard truck. Something strong, to plow the driveway and skid logs. I shopped the classifieds and found one that piqued my interest: a big, old Chevy 4x4, with a 350, four-bolt main. Four-speed with creeper low, and a PTO winch off the transfer case. A beast of a truck—but what an eyesore! No floorboard, just a full view of the ground beneath the truck. The door panels were so rusty that the window glass just fell out the bottom on one side. And let's not talk about the body or paint.

The mechanicals weren't much better. The truck had been parked for 13 years because of a failed clutch. During that time, all four tires had gone flat. It had no exhaust system, no alternator, and no air filter. Hmmm. Was I up for such a risky purchase? He wanted $800. I knew it was worth more than that in parts. But I wanted a running vehicle, not to sell parts. I offered him just $300 as my best price. I apologized that I could not offer more, but had to stick with that. I then tossed the phone number and put the ball in his court. Actually, I was simply entrusting the whole venture to the Lord. I knew that if he called me and accepted my low bid, God would help me get it running again.

Several weeks later, the old man called and accepted the $300 sale. I showed up that weekend with a trailer. We put air in the tires and they held up, but the huge wheels were too wide to fit on the trailer. The seller then emerged from his shed with five regular-sized tires on rims. Not only that, but out came the full, perfect-condition dual exhaust system. In fact, he kept coming out—eventually, with every missing part, and spares to boot. We gathered everything and went home.

I replaced the clutch and reassembled the truck. I poured a little gas in the carburetor and, amazingly (after sitting for 13 years) it fired up immediately. *All the parts were there and they all worked!* Weeks later, when my son, Jonah, was born with several birth defects, that phrase would become one of the most pivotal statements in my Christian walk. But at the time I had no idea what lay ahead.

I ran the truck hard for five good years and ultimately sold it in good running condition (in spite of its ugliness) for $800.

As you can see with this particular example, sometimes you hear from God when you test the waters and give Him room to speak. When you do, the answer to the vital question—*was it Him or was it me?*—becomes self-evident because He does something that only He can do. In this case, I was not certain whether or not the truck purchase was His will, so I gave Him ownership. I knew that if I pursued it with my own logic, my bias in the matter may have led to the wrong decision. It was my "put out my fleece" moment—you know, like when Gideon was facing the Midianites and Amalekites for battle (Judges 6:36-40). And when God took over (as He did in the case of Gideon), I eagerly expected a favorable outcome.

As you see Him follow through with what you surmised was His voice, you train yourself to discern His voice with a higher degree of accuracy. As your faith rises, you will hear Him speak and see Him move with greater and greater frequency. As you grow in this way, stepping out in faith becomes easier. You will eagerly expect God to do what He says—and according to your faith will it be done unto you.

God will also speak through visions. These are different from dreams in that (perhaps obviously) they occur when you are awake. In the summer of 2005 God gave me an unexpected vision of central Indiana. Immediately in my spirit, I knew He was telling us to move there. *But why Indiana?*, I thought. We had neither friends nor family there. Cindy and I had only ever known New England. In time, however, all these details would be sorted out. I simply waited, and the pieces of the puzzle began to fall into place.

When I returned to work after my leave of absence, I negotiated working from home. That allowed me to move clear across the country without finding new employment. Shortly after the vision, God urged us to leave our fellowship of seven years to seek out an alternative. We went slowly, and on good terms, as we both had leadership responsibilities. In the seven-month interim between the change in church and the final move, God introduced the concept of home fellowship to us. We would go west with that paradigm in mind, ultimately planting a fellowship in Indiana.

Our house was on the market for several months. I was away on a business trip in late August when, unbeknownst to me, a couple drove by our home and invited themselves in for an impromptu showing. Cindy, home alone with five children, gave them a tour as the baby screamed in her bouncy seat and the preschooler and toddler strewed their books and toys across the living room. In spite of the chaos, she was somehow sure these people would make an offer on the house. At the same time, hundreds of miles away, the Lord told me that I needed to take the last week of September and the first week of October off to move, because a buyer would make an offer soon. I called my employer and requested the time off. She asked if I had received an offer yet. I told her, "No," but that I felt the Lord showing us that it was imminent.

Talking to Cindy that night, she told me of the unexpected visit and said she was sure that these were the people who would buy our home. She was surprised to learn that I had already requested time off for the move. Days after the showing, we indeed received a full-price offer. We closed on our home September 28, and on our Indiana home the following day.

This example highlights a couple of other ways God speaks. Visions are His way of really getting our attention. Yet, I suppose it is human nature to simply doubt it is from Him or to second-guess the intended purpose. Step out in the small things and grow in discernment so you will be poised and ready to respond to His leading when potentially confusing messages emerge.

The other extremely important tool God used here is *confirmation*. God will normally speak to the decision-maker, the one in authority to act, directly. However, He will often confirm His messages through others (although personally, I would receive a prophetic word from an outside party with some skepticism, unless I had heard from the Lord myself beforehand).

When confirmations do come, they will certainly give you confidence to move forward. As in this case, when He repeats a message to both a husband and wife, He builds and maintains unanimity for any change that will result. God did this for Cindy and me for our big moves: New England to Indiana, and America to Africa.

"Your job will be taken away in December. But don't fear. It is just time for you to be thrust from the nest."

That was the message from the Lord in late August of 2008. I asked my employer if my job was threatened, and I was assured that there were no problems at that time, or in the foreseeable future. Yet I was not surprised when they called me in late November to tell me that because of the economic downturn, they could no longer retain me. I was released the first week of December.

At about the same time, I was invited to teach in Kenya. I accepted and was enthusiastically welcomed, as were the harder teachings I was bringing. During one evening in Western Kenya, God gave me a vision that our family would be moving to Kenya. I called Cindy that night, and before I could even get the words out, she exclaimed, "We are moving to Kenya, aren't we?" She had already received the same message.

Again, God had blessed us both with clear confirmation that He was indeed the author of the enormous life change we were about to embark on. Just imagine how difficult it would have been to endure all the opposition we would receive from loved ones and doubters, had God not given us both complete clarity on His will for the future of our family. God was very gracious to us. And He would provide many more convincing illustrations and guidance to prepare us for the big change ahead.

Cindy describes one such instance of God speaking to her during the transition (excerpted from *The Kingdom of God is Not about Eating and Drinking*):

> Moving from Connecticut to Indiana—what a transition for me in so many ways! I had to remember that a *bag* is a *sack* and people don't have tag sales, they have yard or garage sales. Likewise, when you go to the bank, the kids might get a *sucker*, not a *lollipop*. On my first solo trip to Wal-Mart, I had a screaming baby in the back seat wanting to nurse and I managed to get myself lost off the wrong exit with no idea of how to get home. I couldn't even find a place to pull over to attend to the baby! Navigating my way around took some time. As well, our first six months were spent feeling quite lonely away from our old home fellowship. Any time you move, change is the result and I wouldn't hesitate to say that if we cooperate with God, He uses it for a growth experience. Our journey to Indiana was no exception.
>
> However, after a year, then two...then five, Indiana was *home*. I remember one day, not long after we first talked about moving to Africa, I was returning from visiting a friend. We had just experienced a torrential rain and it was not unusual to find water across the road

between corn fields. Usually the puddles were passable, but sometimes you had to turn around and back-track to find another way to your destination. I was on a back road (a short cut that I preferred) and suddenly found myself face-to-face with a large puddle. With the clearance of our van, I figured there would be no problem getting through it, though I did stop and take a look at the depth of the water before I proceeded. I made it to the other side without any problem. However, not another twenty feet down the road, there was a much larger, longer puddle. In fact, it wasn't a puddle—the road was completely flooded. And it wasn't stagnant water, it was *moving*. I stopped and got out of the van, but even after careful scrutiny I couldn't discern the depth of the dark and foreboding water. Assessing my options, I realized that to turn around now was impossible. There was tall corn on either side of the road and no shoulder to maneuver our large van, even for a 10-point turn. I thought about backing up, but there was no side road in sight. How long could I travel in reverse, and where would I turn around even if I did? There seemed no other option but to move forward—but I was more than nervous.

I literally felt *fear* grip my insides as I re-started the van and my front wheels hit the water—slowly enough that the high water wouldn't splash up into the wheel wells but fast enough that I had some good momentum and wouldn't get bogged down. I was surprised and relieved (after what seemed like forever but was probably only a few minutes) to make it safely to the other side.

The Lord used this experience for me, personally, as an analogy of our moves: first (the small puddle), the sometimes-challenging transition from Connecticut to Indiana; then, the larger and scarier jump coming up, from Indiana to Africa. On the one hand, I felt fearful in contemplating the depth and length of that second puddle, knowing what it would mean in actual experience. On the other hand, I felt confident in the outcome because I knew that God had given me this illustration to show me His hand and offer me His peace. Although I don't know if we're through the water just yet, I remain hopeful of what we'll experience when we get to the other side—and I know that the Lord has already gone ahead of us.

Just like Indiana brought certain changes, Africa has as well. We've had to learn our way around, just as in any other move. I am thankful to the Lord for how He prepared us, and for how He spoke to my heart personally before we finally made the jump into the deeper waters.

Cindy's story illustrates another one of the many methods God uses to speak to His children: analogies. He takes something right in front of you, or in your past, and the Holy Spirit connects it to a seemingly unrelated thing in your life to teach you or show you something.

A beautiful pond on my property? A dream—literally, a dream—come true! In another illustration of hearing from God, early on in my walk I learned that God speaks through dreams, and brings them to fruition—often, not in the way we expect.

We had never intended to purchase Cindy's childhood home. But when I received a promotion with a commensurate pay increase and our family was growing, we capitulated to her father's wish. Shortly after settling into the new home, we were hiking the trails in our backyard. We ended up on our neighbor's property and happened upon their beautiful, man-made pond. Fully stocked with fish, it was a sight to see.

Some years later, I had a dream about a pond, but not on our neighbor's land. Rather, it was in my own backyard. I saw it in the dream, but knew in reality that the place where the pond had been actually overlapped onto my neighbor's property in a densely forested area. Not to mention, such a project was a financial impossibility for us at that time. I just shelved the dream deep into the recesses of my mind. That is, until...

One day the boys and I were fishing at the neighbor's pond and, out of nowhere, he said, "You know, you have a great pond site on the backside of your property." I conceded that this was true, but commented that a portion of that land actually belonged to him. He responded, "I'll give it to you."

Whoa! Could that dream really have been from the Lord? But how could I pay for such a thing? As I meditated on the possibility, the Spirit gave me assurance that the Lord would make the dream a reality. I could not fathom how, but knew it with certainty.

My neighbor's driveway was on an easement through my land, something he had always wanted to change. My neighbor, being a licensed surveyor, worked with me to move our property lines in an even exchange: driveway for pond property. A real win-win, and a free survey to boot. Wetlands permitting went through effortlessly, and again, was free. Remember the beater truck I had picked up? With it, I slowly cleared the forested area, skidding felled trees with the truck and either giving them away or burning them on-site. The last obstacle was the actual machine work.

My neighbor was so pleased with his pond site that he really wanted me to use the same contractor that he had. Because he'd been so cooperative with the whole project, I really tried. But the operator was an old man now and would not do the job. Well, a crazy idea crossed my mind. *What if I made the pond?* I searched eBay for a suitable machine and found a perfect excavator not far from our home. When I looked at it online, my spirit said *yes*, but my mind said, *you have to be joking*! I prayed it up and gave it to the Lord. I decided that if it looked and ran perfectly and I could pick my price, then I would trust God for it.

I looked at the machine, and it was perfect. I picked my price and he accepted it. Oh dear! Was I ready for this? I bought it: a 64,000-pound excavator with an 11-foot stick and over 25-foot digging radius. I signed the check, collected the papers, and organized shipment the coming week. But God had something much different in mind.

After thinking about it the next day, I was very heavily burdened in my spirit to cancel the deal. But I was absolutely confused at this point, because I had felt sure that I was hearing from God and walking by faith. Could I really have been mistaken? Yet I simply could not shake the feeling that I was supposed to cancel. I called the bank and asked if I could stop payment on the check. They said, "No problem."

I called the seller, apologizing profusely, and offered him something for his trouble. He was happy. *Phew*, the Lord had prevented a supposed big mistake. However, this proved to be a huge blow to me spiritually. I felt that I now could not continue to trust the Lord's leading in such matters. My spiritual radar was all confused.

Two months later, Cindy came to me with a bank statement. The check had been cashed. *What*? The bank said they had stopped payment! I called the bank and they were in crisis mode, accepting complete responsibility for their error. I was at ease, assuming that now things would work out just fine, but I asked them if I could negotiate with the other party to set the matter to rest. He was a nice guy and we all figured that he would simply return the funds. Thankfully, he agreed to do just that.

One week went by, then two. No money. And then he stopped answering his phone. After four weeks, I relayed the information to the bank. Suddenly, they claimed no responsibility. *Now what do I do*? I asked the Lord. He responded with absolute clarity, "Nothing! Just wait."

I had no excavator, no paperwork (because I had shipped it back to the seller), and I was down a lot of money—and I was supposed to do *nothing*? *God, you have to be kidding me*, I thought to myself. But He insisted He was in control of the situation and I should not worry. It didn't help. I worried! But I did wait—a long, weary month of waiting. Then suddenly, God gave me a detailed plan of action.

I won't bore you with the details, but suffice it to say, when God finally began to reveal His plan for rectifying this situation, I followed His instructions. Some of it didn't make much sense to me, and I had no idea why He had seemed to say, "Yes," but then, "No," or especially why the prolonged wait had been necessary. Yet in the end, remarkably, the deal drastically changed in my favor and as a result, the pond God had showed me in a dream was completely *free*! And as only God could, He showed me exactly why things had happened as they did.

From this experience, I learned that God's paths are not always straight. His plans are not always self-evident. He is, indeed, in control of all things, but He sees around corners and into the future. He must be trusted and obeyed with all patience, even if the step in front of us is confusing to our human minds.

This situation reminds me of when Paul attempted to go to Asia to preach the kingdom and was stopped by the Holy Spirit (just how, we don't know). A second time, he was again prevented by the Spirit of Jesus, but was ultimately given the go-ahead through a night vision of a man in Macedonia. The result of his obedience to God's leading was the salvation of Lydia and her household, and the Philippian jailer and his household—the very first converts in Asia (see Acts 16).

Though over time I expected to hear from God through His Word, through analogies, and through dreams, I was still a bit surprised the first time He directly spoke to my spirit. It was a normal Thursday morning commute to work in Manchester traffic into East Hartford. Traffic was bumper-to-bumper, traveling at a brisk 30 miles per hour. Then the Lord spoke to my spirit, very clearly, "You are going to be in an accident." *What*? Was it God, or just thoughts in my head? Moments later, still in locked-down traffic, I heard, "Brace yourself, it is about to happen." Again, "Slow down." Three messages in rapid succession. I could no longer doubt it was real. *But I am already going slow. How can I go slower*? I did it anyway, leaving a couple car lengths between me and the car in front of me.

I noted an on-ramp with slowly merging traffic approaching. I suspected someone might come into my lane from there. But suddenly, out of the breakdown lane, a red Jeep Grand Cherokee approached rapidly, but had no room to continue on his trajectory because of the merging traffic. He was forced to careen into my lane, right where I had left the open space. God had just guided me to avoid a wreck. I was dumbfounded. I arrived at work and emailed Cindy the amazing story. Little did I know how significant this event would prove in the coming days when my son, Jonah, was born.

Though this was the very first time God communicated with me directly, it was still a far cry from a voice from Heaven. It was very challenging for me to accept. But luckily for me, He was persistent and repeated the message multiple times. As a result, I believed sufficiently to act upon His message.

In any instance of hearing from the Lord, note that the Holy Spirit will not conflict with the written Word. (For example, you will not receive a revelation or confirmation from God to divorce your lawful, covenant spouse and enter into a forbidden remarriage.)

Hearing from God is essential in our personal walk with the Lord, but more than that, all the revelatory gifts by which He works within the body of Christ—discernment, prophecy, tongues, dreams, visions and words of knowledge—are contingent upon the faith that comes by hearing. Competing thoughts, such as doubt, confusion, and double-mindedness, will create a din that will drown out His quiet voice.

Many say these gifts ceased after the apostles. However, history teaches otherwise. It was evident to the second century church that the gift of prophecy was transferred from the Jews to the Christians.[xxxiii] And the early church simply appealed to the Scriptures themselves to demonstrate that prophecy was an ongoing manifestation within the church.[xxxiv]

House church folks (like myself) almost unanimously ascribe to the New Testament practice of an interactive service. This is based on 1 Corinthians 14:26 which says, "When you assemble, each one has a psalm, has a teaching, has a revelation, has a tongue, has an interpretation. Let all things be done for edification." This describes how God communicates with, and through, individuals for the benefit of the body.

Paul goes on to explain that contributors to the service are to speak one by one, that tongues are to be interpreted, and that prophecy is to be sought because it edifies the entire church. Note that the leader of this service is not a man, but rather the Holy Spirit. The purpose of the interactive service is not to hear the wisdom of men, but rather to hear from God. Yes, we worship and pray to the Lord; however, the emphasis of the corporate fellowship time is on hearing from Him. Unfortunately, our structures and traditions seriously inhibit this dynamic. Not only are most participants in church services silenced, but so is God. Yet the corporate demonstration of the gifts is a vital means by which God speaks to His people. Whether the gifts are used in fellowship or in individual circumstances, they operate the same.

Discernment is a gift of the Spirit that has an important function within the Body. When seeing, talking to, or praying for someone, I often find that specific ideas or images come into my mind. If this happens to you, test and see if it is from God. For example, in the case of the woman in whom I had discerned a spirit of death/suicide, I asked her directly to confirm, and through this God continued to guide our interaction. As with all gifts of faith, you must step out in it when you receive it from the Lord, or it will not grow stronger. This particular gift is powerful in the church for identifying strongholds and the associated unclean spirits so that people can be delivered from specific areas of bondage.

Word of knowledge, which is similar to prophecy, is another means by which God will speak. When God gives you a word concerning someone, it is usually meant to be shared. Step out in faith. However, until you have a proven track record, test yourself for accuracy. For example, if you have a premonition of something happening, wait and see if it comes to pass. Share with people privately, especially if the subject matter is personal in nature. Prophecy and words of knowledge are not areas of gifting for me, so I have little else to share from experience.

Remember with all these means of God communicating with us, we are still people, and the mind may confuse the spirit. Complete accuracy should not be expected unless you have experience in hearing from God and are strong in your faith. Even then, don't get totally deflated if you are "off" here or there. Dust yourself off and keep pressing on. Just because you misunderstand or add to a message once, does not mean that all prior or subsequent messages are suspect. But do be very reluctant to add to a message, "the Lord said," unless you know with certainty what He wants you to share. It is better just to state the facts: what you saw, heard, or discerned, and by what means.

The Holy Spirit gives gifts that are to be exercised for the edification of the Church, but most gifts require the ability to commune with, and hear from, God. He still speaks in many ways to those who have faith to hear Him.

Jesus says His sheep know His voice (John 10:27), so you should not be surprised when you hear it. God may speak through Scriptures, signs, thoughts, or analogies that He knows you will find meaningful. You may receive dreams or visions. At times when it is needed, the messages you hear will come with confirmation. In order to become an effective soldier for the King, you must listen for His voice so that you can understand and act upon His orders. In the next chapter, we'll talk about prayer and fasting, means by which you can jump-start hearing more clearly from our Commander-in-Chief.

Chapter 11—Lines of Communication: Prayer and Fasting

You never know what to expect at *kesha*—that is, an all-night prayer meeting. But I have learned to anticipate surprises. This meeting was no different.

The young woman was deathly ill. She had not eaten anything substantial for a month. A stomach problem kept her from keeping food down, so when I met her she was a shell of her former self—basically skin and bones. Of course, she was terribly weak. In this condition, one can only patiently wait to breathe their last. But God had a different plan.

Mid-way through the prayer meeting, it was her turn to be prayed for. James, a middle-aged man of humble stature, with confidence well beyond his appearance, stepped forward to engage in prayer. We all prayed in unison for God to show up with a miracle. As if out of nowhere, Christine—newly Spirit-baptized and evidently on a mission—hovered around the young girl while forcefully praying in tongues. Her eyes were clenched shut; there was no way she could see what she was doing. Yet she honed in right where needed with precision, slowly making her way between brother James and the sickly young woman. She gently touched the young woman here and there all over her body while praying unceasingly. Suddenly, the girl went down as if dead. Undaunted, Christine kept praying as James stood watching and franticly checking for signs of life, obviously concerned for the woman's well-being. It took a very long five minutes of praying for deliverance and healing before the girl came to, responding to James's gentle slaps on her cheeks.

The young woman was helped into a chair and then she spoke, clearly and with surprising energy: "Do you have something to eat?" She actually *wanted* food for the first time in a very long time. She received a small meal and drink, and later testified to complete healing from that time forward.

We are at war. Every advance we make (salvation, deliverance, or healing) is a direct, frontal attack on the kingdom of darkness. The enemy will not sit idle as we take ground. He will fight back, and we must be prepared for his counter-attack.

Not long after Christine began to step out in faith to do the work of God in healings such as this, she and her husband found themselves under a significant attack of the enemy. In the interest of their privacy, I don't want to divulge the specific details, but they were severely tested in their marriage. Although they were being lifted up in prayer by others during this difficult time, Christine admitted that she found herself unable to pray. It took many months for them to gain the victory, but Christine acknowledged that just one of the reasons for the prolonged trial was that she was not alert and faithful in prayer.

One of the ways that enemy forces seek an advantage during war time is to cut off communication between a commander and his troops. Without effective command and control, they are much more likely to secure a victory. In the same way, our spiritual enemies very often gain an advantage when our essential communication is cut off from our Commander, Jesus Christ. Two ways in which we connect to God in the battle are prayer and fasting. I believe our enemy actively works to disrupt us in these areas, and unfortunately, we are often unaware of his tactics.

In my fellowship circle, the brethren are non-resistant. Consistent with Jesus's teachings to not resist evil-doers and to love our enemies, we do not fight others, even in self-defense. I concede that most Christians do not subscribe to this historic understanding of Jesus' teaching on non-resistance; however, I see multitudes in nearly every sect of Christianity subscribe to non-resistance when it comes to the Devil. Satan prowls around like a roaring lion, and precious few fight back.

Jesus was sent to set the captives free and destroy the works of the devil (Luke 4:18, 1 John 3:8). Then He gave that same authority to the twelve, the seventy, and now every successive generation of disciples until His return at the end of the age. The promised gift, the baptism of the Holy Spirit, gives us power to do that work. We were intended to fight the enemy with every weapon at our disposal.

The example of the Israelites, which was given for us Christians (see 1 Corinthians 10:1-11), shows us that they did not immediately enter into the Promised Land upon being saved from Egypt. In fact, they wandered through the wilderness for 40 years. In the historic account recorded in the books of Exodus and Joshua, we see that they did not receive their reward without a fight. In the same way, we do not immediately inherit God's heavenly kingdom, but rather remain here on Earth as sojourners. Just like the Israelites, we also will fail to inherit the kingdom unless we are prepared for, and engaged in, the fight.

Our Uganda property is filled with snakes, and I'm often reminded that this was the form that Satan chose when he first tempted our forefathers back in the Garden—and that was the beginning of our battle against the spiritual forces of evil. One day, a black mamba and a black forest cobra were sunning on the path when my son, Isaiah, spotted them. Jonah saw the sudden movement and quickly joined in the chase. Always armed with his trusty cane, he made a run for the cobra, who wasted no time in retreating into the marsh grass. Jonah lost sight of it time and again, but luckily it kept peering over the marsh grass with its hood spread as it bolted towards freedom. Jonah gained on him and reached striking distance. *Whack! Whack! Whack, whack!* Jonah stunned him, but could not finish him on the soft muck. Isaiah grabbed the very much living serpent by the neck and carried the flailing beast a couple hundred meters to our home, as the snake kept trying to pry his neck back and inflict a fatal strike. Spying the ordeal from the veranda, I already had a machete in hand and was prepared to administer the death blow. Isaiah placed the cobra on a block of wood and...*chop*, off with his head.

That was just one of seven deadly cobras we have killed on our Uganda property (and several mambas also). These animals are not naturally aggressive; however, when people or livestock stumble upon them unawares, the result may be sudden death. Our property is frequented not only by my own children at play but also by innumerable neighbors, as it is the only nearby lake access for fetching water, doing laundry, launching boats, and fishing. Since anti-venom is not available, such dangerous snakes must be controlled.

The natives look on with awe as my boys fearlessly handle these deadly animals. Their typical response is to run *away* from, not *towards*, the beasts. Of course, they fear them terribly. They just can't understand how these youth can get close enough to kill them with a short cane or a machete.

This simple example is a fitting analogy of our spiritual fight. Jesus gave us authority to trample serpents and scorpions, clarifying that they represent the powers of darkness (Luke 10:19). A serpent can't strike when you are on the chase and he is on the run. However, when you are not attentive to his presence and he is able to roam freely, you can be caught off-guard and struck dead. In the same way, when you are on the offensive, through prayer and intercession, your enemy is on the run and simply seeking self-preservation. He is at your mercy, because you are operating under Christ-given authority. He can do you no harm (Luke 10:19). However, when you are complacent and ignorant of his presence, he can catch you by surprise and inflict great damage.

There have been many books written about prayer, so I don't feel it necessary to elaborate too much on certain aspects of this essential spiritual discipline. I will just offer a few points for your consideration and leave you to explore the subject further on your own, should you so desire.

Prayer is not just a means of presenting our requests to God and getting answers about the things that concern us. If you pray, I mean *really* pray, it will mobilize you to get active on the mission and participate in what God is doing. You can see this happen when the disciples gathered together to pray: the Holy Spirit fell at Pentecost, and they went out in dramatic fashion to witness about Jesus. In Acts 4:29-31, the church prayed again and all were filled with the Holy Spirit and boldness for further work. With action comes reaction; Satan counter-attacks. We, in turn, pray for deliverance. When delivered, we worship and praise and are emboldened to further action. It just keeps going (see Acts chapter 16 for another great example). However, the cycle starts, and continues, with prayer.

If you recall my testimony, the impetus for the re-lighting of the fire of the Holy Spirit in our mission was prayer and fasting. The Kenyan brethren buckled down with all-night prayer meetings, and I embarked on an extended fast with continual prayer. That meditative beginning led to action. As God did His work, Satan responded with a counter-offensive. We continued in prayer and saw God's hand in victory. The cycle continues to this day, and the war rages on.

Another incident in our Uganda home became an apt illustration of the importance of being on the alert and ready to engage in the battle. There were dozens and dozens of mosquitoes: on the ceiling, on the walls, on our net. Just one hour before, there had only been five or six—and I had killed all of them and closed up the room. The door was shut. The window is screened and sealed. I had checked under the bed. So where did these many dozens of mosquitoes come from?

I called Jonah into the room and we began the arduous task of killing every last mosquito with our racket bug-zappers. Then I lit not one, but two mosquito coils and placed them in the room. But I wasn't done. I knew this was more than just insects; this was spiritual. I got on my knees and prayed for God's protection.

Cindy was pregnant with our tenth child. We had already experienced four miscarriages since moving to Africa, at least one definitively from malaria. We were simply trying to cope with the sudden onslaught of mosquitoes, knowing the risk they posed. We were not going to give up another child without a fight. But how do we fight a virtually unseen enemy?

Through this incident, the Lord showed me that although we don't fear mosquitoes, the "little things" must be attended to as much as the bigger ones (like snakes). Mosquitoes are tiny, defenseless, slow-flying bugs that don't even sting. Although the itch of their bite is annoying, they don't inflict pain. However (at least here in Africa), they carry death within them. In fact, malaria-carrying mosquitoes are responsible for more deaths annually than any other animal.

When we are awake, what do we do? We kill them: with our hands, a fly swatter, a racket-zapper and sprays of all kinds. We don't run from them like we would an armed man or even a hostile wasp. We approach them with courage and confidence, because we are of far superior strength. And they know it. When they see us coming, they flee. Very few people will die from a mosquito when the intended victim is alert and vigilant. So how are these pathetic little critters able to kill so very many people? They find you when you are asleep or inattentive.

Though the devil prowls around like a roaring lion, looking for someone to devour, if you simply resist him, he will flee (1 Peter 5:8-9). But what do you suppose will happen if you are not alert, watchful, or attentive to his plans? That's right—you will be lunch! He is relentless and always active. He is seeking to steal, kill, and destroy. But Jesus commands us to remain alert, to keep watch, and not to be found sleeping.

One thing I learned from the Kenyans that is little understood and seldom practiced among Westerners is the *kesha*. The word *kesha* in Swahili actually means to be alert, watchful, or attentive. It is the same word used to describe a commonly-practiced African Christian tradition, the all-night prayer meeting. If you do a word study of "watch" or "alert" in your New Testament, you will see the emphasis given to this concept. You will note night-time prayer as well.

Jesus stayed up and prayed all night before choosing the twelve apostles (Luke 6:12-13). He also prayed all night with Peter, James, and John prior to the crucifixion (Matthew 28:38-41). Paul and Silas were singing and praying at midnight when the earthquake hit in Philippi (Acts 16:25). The brethren were up praying in the middle of the night when Peter was imprisoned (Acts 12:12).

Jesus said to *watch* so as not to fall into temptation, because the spirit is willing but the flesh is weak (Matthew 26:41). He further cautioned his disciples to watch out for the leaven of the Pharisees and Herod (Mark 8:15): religiosity, hypocrisy, and worldliness. John warned us to *watch* so that we do not lose what we have accomplished and we receive our full reward (2 John 8). Paul said to be alert and sober, and to not sleep like others (1 Thessalonians 5:6). He also taught us to put on the full armor of God (Ephesians 6:10-17), saying: "With all prayer and petition pray at all times in the Spirit, and with this in view, be on the alert with all perseverance and petition for all the saints" (Ephesians 6:18). Peter said to be alert, because the devil is on the prowl to get us, and we must resist him (1 Peter 5:8-9). Leaders are to watch over the souls of the saints (Hebrews 13:17); in fact, both *pastor* and *bishop* mean shepherd and overseer—those who watch over the flock.

Jesus said to be watchful and alert for His coming, for He will return like a thief in the night. He said to be dressed for readiness. What do all these admonitions show us? We can't relax in the fight; otherwise, we will be like the unprepared virgins without oil, or like the unfaithful servant. We must be vigilant soldiers, engaged in the battle according to the orders given by our King and Commander. The best way we remain engaged and listen for our orders is through ongoing prayer.

The early church understood the battle that rages. They knew that Satan and his demons could get to us if we fail to remain alert to his devices. They knew that our fight was in personal holiness and constant prayer:

> We do not, then, deny that there are many demons upon earth, but we maintain that they exist and exercise power among the wicked, as a punishment of their wickedness. But they have no power over those who "have put on the whole armour of God," who have received strength to "withstand the wiles of the devil," and who are ever engaged in contests with them, knowing that "we wrestle not against flesh and blood, but against principalities, against powers, against the rulers of the darkness of this world, against spiritual wickedness in high places." (Origen ANF v. 4, 653. c. 248 AD)

The phrase *being dressed in readiness* reminds me of when Nehemiah was building the wall around Jerusalem. The workers remained attentive day and night, always on watch and armed with a weapon. They were workers by day and guards by night. They labored, yes, but were constantly watching and waiting for the trumpet to sound so they could rally together for battle (Nehemiah 4:11-23). The unity of purpose and camaraderie of the Israelites as they worked and watched together is a great example to us of what can be accomplished through our personal, and corporate, prayer efforts and the works in which we engage as a result.

The Bible is full of examples of dramatic answers to prayer; it was all-night-prayer meetings that launched our mission into high gear. The opposite is likewise true: neglecting to pray puts us at risk of loss and defeat in the ongoing spiritual battle. These two opposing truths were illustrated in rapid succession, after two different church members received the baptism of the Holy Spirit.

He was gone; our beloved deacon and faithful friend, dead at 70 years. Burying dearly-beloved brethren is the last thing I was mentally and emotionally ready for when preparing for the mission field. I had never been a pastor of a traditional church stateside, just home fellowships. Therefore, funerals and weddings were all new to me. But since coming to Africa, I had buried several brethren. My minivan had served as a hearse multiple times. But why *Mzee* Moses—and why now?

He had received the baptism of the Holy Spirit just days before his sudden illness. We prayed and prayed, as individuals and as a church, during his lengthy hospitalization. On multiple occasions he was despairing of life, having simply given up. There was no changing his mind; he had prepared to die. The visions and prophecies, even visible evidence, all suggested witchcraft. Yet despite the ongoing prayer effort, there was no evidence of breakthrough.

The night of Moses' death, we had a regularly-scheduled *kesha*. Under such terrible circumstances, prayer was not something I could neglect. At the meeting, Richard (a visiting prophet from another fellowship) warned that several people close to me would die. They would simply grow ill and suddenly be gone. Little did he know that *Mzee* Moses had died just two hours prior to our prayer gathering.

When alone with Richard later, I asked him why Satan would be able to get to the people around me, but not me. He answered without hesitation: "Because you pray!" I took in what he was saying deeply. I knew Moses was the very best of men, as far as honesty, personal character, and holiness. However, I also noted he was, indeed, not a praying man. You would never find him attending an all-night prayer meeting. To my knowledge, he had never fasted. Those activities were normal for our evangelists and select intercessors, but not our dear deacon. I couldn't help but give credence to Richard's words, and his warning.

Around the same time, Ellen in Uganda became deathly ill, also immediately after receiving the baptism of the Holy Spirit. She very nearly died; her recovery was only because of God's intervention. I couldn't help but note that she *prays*. Satan is threatened by the advancement of the saints from complacency to empowerment. When the enemy sees us acquire this particular weapon, He attacks forcefully.

Following my conversation with Richard, I gathered the saints who work closely with me and advised them that the battle was real, and that they needed to pray more. Two confessed that they were receiving many dreams and visions about their imminent death. We prayed against the spirit of death. Both later reported being freed from these visions and feelings. They in turn recommitted themselves to the fight; that is, to constant prayer. These brothers have not missed a *kesha* since. Resist the devil, and he will flee from you.

These all-night prayer meetings are never disappointing. We routinely see multiple healings, exorcisms, and countless other answers to prayer. God interacts with His people in visions, words of knowledge, prophecies, and dreams. It is an opportunity to invite the Holy Spirit to do spectacular things.

Really Lord? You want me to do what? Okay.

I was having this conversation with God during one of our *keshas*. However, I have this conversation with God more often than I might like. What He was asking of me this time was very public. And me, being very introverted, well—it was a stretch.

"Okay everyone, this is what we will do. The Lord wants us all, as a group, to confess and repent of our sins, declare and renounce our personal and family strongholds, and release and forgive all who have victimized us, here and now. Then I will pray for us all at once."

None of this was new to any of the disciples present. What I was describing is the standard "spiritual inventory" that we go through with anyone who desires to repent and be baptized. What was unique this time was that we would do it publicly, and corporately. With well over 20 people attending this all-night prayer meeting, it would certainly be an experience.

One of the elders, a serious prayer warrior who must have callouses on his knees from praying on them so much, insisted that everyone form a circle, get on their knees on the cement floor, and hold hands during this process. We took our positions and sang a couple songs. We all took a little time to inspect ourselves and pray alone. As confessions began, strongholds were commanded: "Spirit of envy and jealousy go, now, in the name of Jesus. Spirit of anger, go. Spirit of rebellion, spirit of..." In the name of Jesus and by His authority, out they went. One woman was visibly disturbed, a personal spirit clearly manifesting. I moved in closer and prayed for her until she was freed. Her husband also had something removed. In the end, five people testified they were delivered from spirits or strongholds during our time together.

Perhaps the most significant fruit of the *kesha* is the love and unity that has grown among the brethren as we pray together. Those who pray together, stay together—and labor together, and bear one another's burdens. The unity of soldiers in a platoon is not by virtue of wearing the same uniform; it is the result of sharing in the same experiences. The *kesha* is where this sense of brotherhood is most evident as we corporately experience God.

Paul says that the weapons of our warfare are not carnal, but are powerful for the pulling down of strongholds (2 Corinthians 10:4). Fasting is a companion to prayer and can be used to increase its effectiveness. Jesus once said his disciples could not cast out a particular demon because some require prayer *and* fasting (Matthew 17:21).

I recommended fasting in a couple of previous chapters as a means of humbling ourselves, cleansing ourselves, and drawing near to God so that He will draw near to us (James 4:6-10). This should be our posture as we approach God in prayer, so it makes sense that fasting and prayer should go together. The Bible says the prayer of a righteous man is powerful and effective (James 5:16) and that if we ask anything according to His will, He hears us and will respond accordingly (1 John 5:14-15). Fasting can only strengthen us in our pursuit of righteousness and in our discernment of God's will, making our prayers that much more effective.

There is actually no command in the New Testament to fast. However, it is implied that Christians will do so. When questioned by the Pharisees about fasting, Jesus replied that His disciples would fast after He went to the Father (Matthew 9:14-15). He even gave instructions how we should fast—specifically, by not making a show of it (Matthew 6:16-18).

Jesus embarked on an extended fast right before His public ministry (Matthew 4:2). The brethren fasted when Paul and Silas were sent on their apostolic journey (Acts 13:3) and when elders were appointed (Acts 14:3). Paul fasted for three days after his encounter with Christ on the road to Damascus (Acts 9:9) and when he was adrift in the storm (Acts 27:33). Several references from the *Apostolic Constitutions* (compiled c. 390 AD) indicate that the early church corporately fasted, routinely every Wednesday and Friday.

Fasting typically refers to abstinence from food, though Paul denied himself food and water for three days after he was blinded. There is one Old Testament example of the refusal of "choice foods" (Daniel 10:3). The power of fasting is to deny oneself of fleshly appetites in order to hear from God. The Holy Spirit is drowned out by our carnal desires and affections. Paul says the flesh continually wars against the spirit (Galatians 5:17). Denying these competing forces gives the Holy Spirit unhindered control of our vessel.

I personally believe that the spirit and purpose of fasting is not simply to deny the one sense, but rather all the senses, in order for the spiritual senses to be activated. So I advise to likewise deny sex (see 1 Corinthians 7:5), worldly entertainment, and any other distractions that hinder the Spirit's working.

It also seems to me that the New Testament examples of fasting all provide a purpose for the fast, and the fast ends when that purpose is accomplished. In my experience, it is difficult to maintain an extended fast unless I have an objective in mind. As the saying goes, *if you don't know where you are going, how do you know when you get there?* It's the same with fasting. When I have a goal, I persevere until that goal is achieved.

There can be many reasons for fasting: getting closer to God, dealing with personal strongholds, receiving revelation, obtaining a spiritual gift, or simply interceding for a great need. We like to have baptismal candidates fast before they go through the process of spiritual self-examination, because fasting tears down the defenses of unclean spirits and exposes strongholds. This ensures that they approach the baptismal waters in a cleansed state, ready to receive the Holy Spirit. However, the goal of a spiritual fast should never be selfish in nature (i.e., to achieve weight loss, detoxification, or to meet a personal goal of fasting for a certain number of days). Fasting for health reasons is fine, but don't confuse your goals.

I recommend six steps for a successful fast. All revivals—personal, corporate, community, or national—start with repentance, and this is a good place to start in your fast. Confess everything you can think of as far back as you can remember, even if it has already been cleansed by the blood of Christ (at least the first time you do this). Then add the sins of your family. Finally, repent for the sins of your people. Be thorough. The second step is to seek God's presence in worship, perhaps through the Word or through praise. When you draw near to Him, He will draw near to you. Thirdly, listen quietly for His voice. When you hear from Him, be prepared to act upon what you hear. At this point, you should be ready to petition Him concerning the objectives for which you entered the fast. Next, receive from Him any words or answers He may reveal. Believe you have already received your petition, and you already have, especially if you have approached Him as a cleansed vessel and with a seeking heart. You can then close your fast with thanks and praise.

If you want to be an effective, front-line soldier for Christ, you should always pray, and fast with some regularity. When pouring yourself out on the front lines, battling the powers of darkness, you will become spiritually drained and will need to be recharged. Fasting and prayer refill your tank. And if you take any ground for the kingdom whatsoever, expect retaliation from the spiritual forces of evil. Simply pray and fast all the more. It is in your weakness that God is strong against every tactic and plan of the enemy.

Chapter 12—Casualties: Suffering and Persecution

He was crawling down the path to our home; it was pitch black in the middle of the night. On either side of the path he could hear the sounds of growling and the shrieking of fierce beasts. Absolute terror! Then, as if light bulbs suddenly illuminated both sides of the path, angels' shapes took form. There were two rows of angels on either side, clearly marking the path. They were very tall, about ten feet, with wings and gleaming in golden array. They were standing at attention, holding their long swords over the path.

As his confidence increased, he stood and continued walking along the path towards our compound. At one point, he glanced back and saw that one angel was trailing immediately behind him, brandishing a sword over his head in a gesture of protection. Suddenly he was at the front door of our home, and the angels immediately fell into position along our fence-line.

At that moment the gate opened and a sinister man entered our compound. The nearest angel scanned him and picked a handgun from him, removed the bullets, and returned his pistol to him unawares. The man, now effectively disarmed, continued walking towards our home.

This was one of seven dreams in rapid succession that the Lord gave to people close to me at a critical time. Just days prior, on the way to Nairobi to pick up a new family joining us on the mission, I received an ominous text message. It was a warning that the sender had been hired to kill me. I was lying on the bench of the van, nursing malaria sickness as another brother drove. A phone call immediately followed. The man asked if I had received and understood the message. He told me that he and three others had been given thousands of dollars by someone I knew—someone who I knew the day prior had received a large sum of money, someone I knew had motive, someone who I knew did not like me there in the village—in order to kill me. My heart sank. *Really, on the day we are welcoming a new family? The excitement never ends*, I thought to myself.

This deep-voiced African man told me that he called me with an offer. If I would out-do the payment made to him to kill me, he would spare my life. As much as the thought of someone killing me was unappealing, threats and intimidation are a very poor method of motivating me to action. I refused. He told me to think about it.

By text, he asked me again. I did not respond but instead sent him a very small amount of money using a Kenyan mobile pay system. Immediately (as is customary when using this service), I received a confirmation of the payment that told me his name. The man was sent a similar message, informing him of money received. He now knew that I would have a clue to his identity. He sent me a furious text, saying that I may know his name, but that he would finish me very soon. I told him I was on my way to Nairobi and would be home the next day, not wanting him to get to my family while I was out. That made him even angrier. I warned my wife to lock down the compound and release the dog day and night.

When I returned home, we implemented maximum vigilance, though we are non-resistant and do not even advocate self-defense when attacked. We shut down the clinic that was operating in our compound in order to prevent strangers from entering. We let the dog roam freely day and night and kept the gate locked. Though the dog is not trained security, he is an effective deterrent and alarm.

We did not share information with any locals, except one: our most trusted disciple of many years, Chris. I did notify the authorities, but wasn't sure how fruitful that would be. The workers who used an office in our home knew something was amiss, but did not know the specifics. The situation was in the Lord's hands.

We spent the next couple of days quietly, prayerfully waiting. Then, while in town with another brother, Chris was approached by a black SUV with tinted glass. In it were four well-dressed men: two in front, two behind. The driver peered at, of all people, Chris, through the cracked window and asked him where the *mzungu* at [my location] lived. Chris asked the man why he was looking for me. The man harshly replied, "Answer the question and mind your own business!"

Chris forcefully responded, "I'm the *mzungu*. If you want him, you must go through me!" The man was irate. Chris yelled aloud to attract the attention of the few people loitering around, "These men are bad, bad. These men are bad!" Having discerned that they were the hired killers, Chris rallied the crowd, which with surprising speed converged upon the vehicle. The SUV burst forth and turned around rapidly, narrowly making a hasty escape from the convening mob. They were gone, having accomplished little but to learn that their target was not to be a simple one at all.

A couple days later, the Lord gave me a dream. A few of our brethren, wielding tools, converged upon and surrounded a deadly spider—dangerous and poisonous like a black widow, but extremely agile and large like a brown recluse. However, he was far too fast to be taken out. He easily could have gotten one of us, but instead made his escape for cover in a pile of brush near the door inside my veranda. It was obvious there was no safe way to stir him up and get him without injury or loss of life on our side. Then it dawned on me. Simply spray the pile thoroughly with some poison and he will be finished—*done!*

The Lord showed me that the death threat and those connected with it were like that spider—difficult to bring out into the open and equally impossible to overcome. We could only pray and trust God for deliverance—that was the spiritual "spray" that would accomplish what we, in the physical, could not. We did just that. Shortly after, the Lord revealed in my spirit that it was done—He had somehow taken care of the situation. With complete confidence, we immediately restored our lives back to normal and were never contacted or disturbed again.

You can't go to war without casualties. Trials, suffering, and persecution are an ironclad guarantee for anyone engaged in the spiritual battle, because waging war involves engaging enemies. We are plundering enemy territory, recruiting the enemy's citizens, and turning them into traitors of their former master, Satan. We are illuminating them to the truth: that they are not actually free citizens, but really slaves. We are delivering them from their bondage to unclean spirits and sicknesses, setting them on the path to the truth. The enemy does not like our program and will do anything in his power to stop our work. Therefore, we must expect the attack, and pray for our perseverance.

In my time as a front-line soldier I have experienced death threats, robberies, betrayals of the worst kinds, slanders, threats to my family, false accusations, gossip, constant sicknesses, accidents, curses, witchcraft, and I am sure many other things that I have not seen, but from which the Lord has protected us. This is to be expected; Jesus said we are blessed if we are persecuted, for ours is the kingdom (Matthew 5:10-12). He said that we are not above Him, and since they persecuted Him, they will also persecute us (John 15:12). Paul said that it will be through much tribulation that we enter the kingdom of God (Acts 14:22). Peter said not to be surprised at these things, but rather embrace the trials as a testament to our standing in the Spirit and in God (1 Peter 4:12-19). In fact, Peter goes so far as to say we were called for the purpose of sharing in Christ's sufferings and that when we patiently endure hardship, this finds favor with God (1 Peter 2:19-21).

During my second year in Kenya, I was in a serious motorcycle accident. I was on my way to a mission with a translator and was forced off the road at about 70 kilometers per hour, down an abrupt drop-off. It was reported that the bike rolled three times as we were thrown from it. I recall standing up immediately to check if my translator was alright. Three men lifted the bike off of him; he said he was fine, and I immediately went unconscious.

The next thing I knew, I was being carried to a passing car that had been flagged down to serve as my ambulance. They tried to put me in the front seat, but I told them I could not bend my right knee. They put me in the backseat. I was completely incoherent because of the shock, but at a critical intersection I told them the name of a hospital I wanted to go to. This forced them to go to a different hospital in a more distant city, but I thank God, because it likely saved my leg.

As the one-and-a-half hour trip progressed, my wits returned and I now knew what was going on. At the hospital they tried to remove my pants to see my leg. I insisted they cut the pants off; then we all saw the damage. My flesh was torn open in a swath about five inches wide on my knee. All the soft tissue was pulled up as a flap and my bones were visible. This was a surprise to everyone, because no blood ever hit the ground—that is, until they exposed it.

When they inspected the wound and cleaned it, it was more pain than I had ever experienced. Yet the entire time I never ceased praising God, praying, and even singing. My translator, who was still accompanying me, and the medical staff were amazed. An exposed ligament was 50% torn. Surgery was recommended, but it was so painful I told them to close it up; it would have to heal on its own.

While the doctor was stitching me, I prayed in earnest, because he only gave me a dozen or so shots of local anesthetic; however, these went through the dangling flap of flesh but not into the lower flesh. That meant when the doctor installed the oh-so-many stitches, each time that long curved needle did its arc, it pierced tissue that had received no anesthetic whatsoever. OUCH! But I kept praying and praising God.

The location of the wreck was immediately in front of the home of a former member who had been put out of the church because he was a practicing witchdoctor. In fact, I was in a wreck on the same bike at the same location with an injury to the same leg just a week before this incident, yet God had miraculously healed me. There was little doubt that this was witchcraft-related. But God turned the evil for good.

The Lord had showed me before the wreck that He really wanted me to work on a writing project. However, I was doing one or two multi-day missions weekly, rendering me way too busy to get to it. Ironically, He slowed me down. Bed-ridden and unable to walk or ride, I finished the project in exactly twenty days. When I received the flood of visitors over the next couple months, I shared with them that the downtime allowed me to work on something the Lord deemed more important. Therefore, I was praising God for the injury.

The Lord also revealed to me that I would be back on my bike in three weeks. He said, "Just like Jonah was home in three weeks, so you will be back on the mission in three weeks." At the time, we had still not done an x-ray because they wanted to stitch me up first to stop the bleeding. And the condition of my motorcycle was completely unknown. Yet I posted on Facebook (and shared with the disciples) that I would be back on the mission in three weeks. And what happened? In exactly three weeks to the day, I drove my bike solo and taught a three-day pastoral training mission. Many in our fellowship took great encouragement from this testimony and it served as an important reminder of the importance of suffering trials with grace.

Satan is an opportunist. He will seek out the weakest link in the chain in an effort to disable you. If you are weak, he may only need to leverage entertainments, addictions, worldliness, or even business and career success to distract you from the Lord's service. If you have overcome the flesh and the world to any significant degree, he may have to take things to the next level. He can bog you down with sickness, legal encumbrances, relationship problems, fears, doubts, confusion, and the like, to render you ineffective and inconsequential for the kingdom of God.

If these still fail, he attacks the religious with dogmatism, factionalism, self-righteousness, judgment, infighting, divisiveness, and false doctrine (easy-believism and cessationism among the top of the list) to isolate and immobilize the would-be soldiers of Christ. Ideological strongholds are the most powerful and difficult to break because they are strongly held convictions, oftentimes linked to someone's personal, spiritual identity.

Yet if even these various efforts of the enemy are overcome by the Spirit, the enemy does not let up—but now he has to get serious. He will engage the soldiers of Christ directly with persecution in an attempt to deter them. The bad stuff they did to Paul, Peter, John, James, and Stephen become in play; this is what Jesus promised would follow His real disciples.

Slanderous rumors were certainly not new to me years into our mission. In fact, gossip is prevalent in our village and represents just one stronghold through which the enemy often operates very effectively. These idle whispers often feed misinformation and fuel jealousy over supposed benefits offered to select individuals but not others, and so on. Rumors of our fellowships being "devil-worshippers" are common. It is a constant battle.

Every time I am afforded an opportunity to preach at a public event, such as a funeral, I speak the truth so that the enemy can't benefit from the things kept in darkness. People learn firsthand that we actually preach Jesus and His word and expose the lies of the false gospel. Following such events, the buzz in the village is electric. I get reports that people are talking about how they were lied to and that our mission is preaching the truth—the real truth! Yet even with the lies exposed, people hesitate to join us. Strongholds keep them paralyzed for fear of others.

These same people, however, come to get maize if they are in need, which anyone is welcome to do. Our community-based medical program is also not restricted to brethren, but open to all. Satan is not threatened by good works. We can be "good" all we want. You'd likely be able to go to a Muslim-majority country and provide food, medical assistance, clothes, business training, and loans all you want with little disturbance. However, once you directly engage in the spiritual battle according to Jesus' instructions (that is, preach the kingdom, heal the sick, and expel demons in His name), you will see how quickly the enemy escalates things and tries to shut you down.

In the same way, if you call yourself a Christian but are sidelined from the battle by any of the first lines of attack cited above, you may never get to the level of experiencing real persecution. You are already defeated. Why would Satan drop an A-bomb if you retreated at the sight of a pellet gun? Satan will leave you alone as long as you remain disengaged from real warfare, so don't let his tactics sideline you; expect the attack and be ready to fight back!

It had been over five years since I had visited America. It was an exciting event indeed. It was a chance for us to visit family both in Connecticut and in Canada, and do some fruitful ministry. As we were preparing for the trip, a couple folks reached out to me with a sincere desire to take their spiritual lives to the next level. One dear family had reached the end of the line. They had struggles and burdens they just could not seem to get victory over. The brethren they fellowshipped with simply told them to repent, stop this, change that, and they confessed to feeling alienated from the group because they just couldn't seem to get things together well enough. The fellowship had all the right doctrine, or so it seemed, but lacked the practical tools that could bring lasting freedom from the strongholds that held this family in bondage. Well in advance of our trip, I agreed to meet with them and very much looked forward to what God would do when we got together.

As we began our travels, the husband reached out to me with questions and unspecified concerns. It was obvious that someone was trying to dissuade them from meeting with me. In the end, and quite at the last minute, he abruptly canceled the visit. I politely replied that the purpose of my visit was to help them. There was no incentive for me other than to be blessed with participating in their spiritual progress. I saw some irony in the fact that they felt rejected by certain brethren, yet they were willing to shun another brother whose only goal was to help. I shared that observation with him, but afterward let the matter rest.

A day later he called me again. This time, he was clearly confused and torn in his spirit. He had never met me and said he felt awful that he was cancelling because of hearsay. It literally brought him to tears. Through much introspection he decided to re-schedule. The meeting was on.

When I arrived, we immediately hit it off and got to work. In a short time, he recognized the spirit and heart of my intent. I would come to learn that five stateside brethren had been warning him to avoid me. Yet God had different plans. Through many hours of discourse, pouring out of hearts, and prayer, both husband and wife were delivered from their strongholds in Jesus' name. Following that, both received the promised gift of the Father—the baptism of the Holy Spirit.

Our next stop brought us East to another couple seeking deliverance and the baptism of the Holy Spirit. Yet again, these sincere brethren were warned not to associate with me. One slanderous brother told him that people should not even fund our mission, because funds were not used as earmarked. It broke my heart to hear such lies. These brethren warning him were not "outsiders," but were people I had considered true brothers, with belief and practice common to my own.

Yet God again prevailed. This couple would not be swayed. They knew their struggles and knew no one locally who could assist them with their needs. We met and fellowshipped, and in the end, they were also delivered from their strongholds in Jesus' name and received the baptism of the Holy Spirit.

As these examples illustrate, I have come to expect persecution and betrayal, gossip, and slander. These have become the norm in our mission now, and the enemy often uses those closest to me. Yet Jesus promised rejection, persecution, and even betrayal by those whom we love the most. Strongholds are hard to see, that is why Satan uses them so successfully. Religious strongholds are among the most difficult, which is why the Scriptures warn so often against divisions, factions, slander, back-biting, and the like. Front-line battle will always be accompanied by trials of various kinds. We must fix our eyes on Jesus and continue the fight. He is worth it, as are the people we are serving:

> But we have this treasure in earthen vessels, so that the surpassing greatness of the power will be of God and not from ourselves; we are afflicted in every way, but not crushed; perplexed, but not despairing; persecuted, but not forsaken; struck down, but not destroyed; always carrying about in the body the dying of Jesus, so that the life of Jesus also may be manifested in our body. For we who live are constantly being

delivered over to death for Jesus' sake, so that the life of Jesus also may be manifested in our mortal flesh... Therefore we do not lose heart, but though our outer man is decaying, yet our inner man is being renewed day by day. For momentary, light affliction is producing for us an eternal weight of glory far beyond all comparison, while we look not at the things which are seen, but at the things which are not seen; for the things which are seen are temporal, but the things which are not seen are eternal. (2 Corinthians 4:7-11, 16-18)

When we are cursed, we must bless. When we are confronted with evil, we are commanded to overcome with good. As tempting as it is to despair or be discouraged, we are told to rejoice in everything. We pray for our enemies, recognizing that people are not the enemy—the spiritual forces of evil are. As we walk in obedience to our King in the face of suffering, we grow ever-stronger spiritually. The tactics of the enemy accomplish little as we look forward with hope to the eternal reward that will be ours if we persevere through these battles large and small.

Chapter 13—Marching in Step with the King

Every soldier goes through "basic training" and is then sent out to the front lines where ever he will serve. He is expected to follow orders and remain under authority; otherwise, he will find himself released from his duty, often dishonorably. As soldiers of Christ fighting against the domain of darkness, the expectation for us is the same. Our basic training includes the "elementary teachings of the faith" which we have already identified from Hebrews 6: repentance and faith, baptism and the laying on of hands (for receiving the baptism of the Holy Spirit), the resurrection of the dead, and eternal judgment.

Once we master these essentials we are ready to press on to maturity; that is, we acquire experience on the front lines and strive to fulfill the commands of our King, Jesus. Yet it is only as we walk under His authority and in obedience to His words that we remain in honorable service. Many are those who have begun well but have then been deceived by the enemy, either in their personal Christian walk or in their work for the Lord. The apostle Paul challenged the Galatians that, having begun by the Spirit, they were in danger of trying to become perfect through works of the flesh. We can run the same risk if we don't stay in close communion with Christ through prayer and fasting and purpose to respond to all that He reveals to us.

Just as Simon the Sorcerer wanted to buy the gift that the apostles possessed for selfish motives, or like the seven sons of Sceva tried to leverage the name of Jesus to cast out demons, operating in the power of the Holy Spirit can likewise be a temptation for us. We must always remember that it is God's power, not ours, and that we are to serve Him in humility according to His leading, not for the fulfillment of personal motivations.[xxxv]

When Jesus sent out the seventy, they returned with joy, reporting to their Master, "'Lord, even the demons are subject to us in your name.'" Jesus commended them, but left them with a warning as well: "'Do not rejoice in this, that the spirits are subject to you, but rejoice that your names are recorded in heaven'" (Luke 10:17, 20). We are called as soldiers to engage in the battle, and we do so by the power of the Holy Spirit. However, we cannot neglect our primary duty: to maintain fellowship with Christ through the same indwelling Spirit and keep our minds set on things above.

That is why, in this chapter, I thought it of utmost importance to look a little more deeply at the Christian walk: the concept of being not only filled with, but led by, the Holy Spirit, and how to maintain fellowship with God through obedience. I don't want any of you to run the risk of losing all that you have gained thus far.

Hopefully you are somewhat familiar with the Old Testament account of the Israelites' enslavement in Egypt, and how God miraculously freed them from the hand of Pharaoh. In a journey to the Promised Land that should have taken days, the Israelites instead spent 40 years wandering in the wilderness. Why? The short answer is, they were disobedient to their God and quickly forgot how He had worked in power to redeem them from their years of bondage.

We are told three times in the New Testament that their story serves as an example for us Christians (see 1 Corinthians 10:1-11, Hebrews 3:16-4:1, and Jude v. 5). Let's look at just one of those passages and see how it relates to the subject at hand:

> For I do not want you to be unaware, brethren, that our fathers were all under the cloud and all passed through the sea; and all were baptized into Moses in the cloud and in the sea; and all ate the same spiritual food; and all drank the same spiritual drink, for they were drinking from a spiritual rock which followed them; and the rock was Christ. Nevertheless, with most of them God was not well-pleased; for they were laid low in the wilderness. Now these things happened as examples for us, so that we would not crave evil things as they also craved. Do not be idolaters, as some of them were; as it is written, "The PEOPLE SAT DOWN TO EAT AND DRINK, AND STOOD UP TO play." Nor let us act immorally, as some of them did, and twenty-three thousand fell in one day. Nor let us try the Lord, as some of them did, and were destroyed by the serpents. Nor grumble, as some of them did, and were destroyed by the destroyer. Now these things happened to them as an example, and they were written for our instruction, upon whom the ends of the ages have come. (1 Corinthians 10:1-11)

This example perfectly describes the Christian experience. Let's look first at the obvious parallels. Just as the Israelites were enslaved to Pharaoh in Egypt, we were enslaved to Satan, sin, and the world. The Israelites were delivered from death through the blood of the Passover lamb; we were delivered from the law of sin and death through the blood of Jesus, the Lamb of God. Just as they were set free by a deliverer, Moses, we were delivered by Christ. They passed to freedom through the baptism of the sea; we also go from death to life, being born again in water baptism. Just as they ate and drank the spiritual food which is Christ, we also partake in the body and blood of Christ as our spiritual food in the observance of communion. The Israelites were sojourners eagerly awaiting their promised rest, instructed not to store up excess nor call the wilderness home. We, too, are sojourners commanded not to store up treasures on earth, but rather commanded to trust God for our daily bread.

Now let's look at some of the similarities that may not be so obvious. Just like many of the Israelites were saved, but in the end only a couple received what was promised, we are likewise told that the way to life is narrow and there will be "few" who find it—many will be called, but only a few chosen. The Israelites did not enter their rest immediately upon their salvation, but rather wandered in the wilderness for some time. Christians, too, remain in the wilderness of this world, where they must continue in faithfulness so that they will receive their reward. The Israelites received the promise by continually fighting against their enemies and persevering to victory. Likewise, we must fight the spiritual forces in the heavenlies until we, through perseverance, receive our inheritance. Their promise was conditional and was lost upon their disobedience, idolatry, and immorality. We, too, will be cut from the Vine if we fail to bear fruit (see John 15:6). Just as they sat to eat and stood to play, in the same way many Christians live for self-satisfaction and pleasure—the worldliness that prevents fruitfulness (see Luke 8:14).

As you can see, this passage is very instructive as regards our salvation and our Christian walk. It also teaches us about being led by the Holy Spirit. Did you notice that all were baptized "in the cloud *and* in the sea," and not the sea only? The sea obviously compares to our water baptism, but the cloud relates specifically to the baptism of the Holy Spirit and how the Holy Spirit then works in us.

As John the Baptist said, he baptized with water, but Jesus would come and baptize in the Holy Spirit. Jesus also said that to enter the kingdom we must be born of water *and* the Spirit. The Old Testament foreshadowed both of these New Testament truths in the account of the Israelites' deliverance from the Egyptians.

The cloud had three purposes, as does the Holy Spirit[xxxvi]:

1. To shield and comfort them from the desert sun—this represents the work of the Comforter sent to convict, teach, and remind of everything Jesus said.

2. The pillar of fire by night—this foreshadows the Holy Spirit as the power to embolden and gift us to be His witnesses. The Holy Spirit came as tongues of fire, described by John the Baptist as "the Holy Spirit and with fire" and explained by Jesus as being power sent by the Father for them to be God's witnesses.

3. The third work of the cloud was to lead them by day, as the Holy Spirit was sent to lead and guide with His gentle wind. The Israelites moved when the cloud moved, following its lead; when the cloud stopped, they made camp. Similarly, we are to walk by the Spirit, and not by the flesh. We are to follow the Holy Spirit's lead in our time as sojourners in this world. He is our teacher and guide.

Although the Israelites were freed from Egypt through the cloud and the sea, they still struggled with having Egypt in their hearts as they wandered in the wilderness. They complained against God, wanting foods that they favored in Egypt, and so on. In spite of the mighty works that God performed on their behalf, their strongholds persisted and many fell in the wilderness. In the same way, Christians are warned they will not inherit the kingdom of God if they continue walking in the deeds of the flesh rather than by the Spirit (Galatians 5:16-19, Ephesians 5:5-6, 1 Corinthians 6:9-10).

What does it mean to walk by the Spirit? Thus far, we've really only talked about the power of the Holy Spirit that equips us as His witnesses and as soldiers for Christ, and a bit about remaining connected to Him through prayer and fasting. There has, as yet, been little emphasis given to the Spirit's work of conviction of sin and righteousness, and reminding us of everything Jesus taught. These are important functions that have everything to do with walking by the Spirit, which can be simplified as *holiness*, or being set apart for God.

He is indeed called the *Holy* Spirit for a reason. He leads us toward greater and greater holiness, for the Scriptures warn that without such holiness, no one will see God (Hebrews 12:14). Unlike His original work of conviction of sin and deliverance that starts us on the path, the walk of holiness is ongoing and must continue if we are to remain in God's honorable service as soldiers.

The demonstrations of power accomplished by the authority of the name of Jesus are not necessarily the same as spiritual gifts or the fruit of holiness, so as I have already warned, do not judge men's teachings based on the wonders they perform. Instead, look at their fruit—particularly, the fruit of the Spirit or the fruit of holiness that is (or is not) evident in their lives. Fruitless wonders may impress men, but the Lord is not deceived. He will reject those lawless ones on the last day (Matthew 7:21-23).

Those lawless ones are the main reason that Satan has been so effective at convincing people that these wonders are counterfeit and that this work of the Holy Spirit is not to be believed in this day and age. Our human minds simply have trouble reconciling how sinners and false teachers can operate in power, unless the source is demonic or the wonders are completely fraudulent. Charismatics often demonstrate the power of the Spirit and bring teachings about His works, but they don't realize that by their fruit (the failure to evidence personal holiness) the gifts of God may fall into disrepute. The onus is upon us to continually walk in victory and holiness, so as to expose Satan's lies and not to dishonor Christ.

Being cleansed from sin (accomplished through the blood of Christ) and gaining freedom from strongholds are two different processes, so it's important not to misidentify the origin of our struggles. People are quick to label others as prideful, rebellious, angry, bitter, and so on, and a call to repentance usually follows. *Actions* can be repented of, but *spirits* cannot. We need to take responsibility for sin: confess, be cleansed, and repent (change) with the help of the Holy Spirit. Yet if the problem is an impersonal spirit and not a specific sin, victory comes in a very different way. These spirits need to be renounced, and we need to be delivered from their power. This only comes as we identify and uproot this work of the enemy completely. Ongoing vigilance and discipleship in the renewing of the mind are necessary to prevent their recurrence.

Maybe you're like I was when I first picked up the New Testament; I read Jesus' words, "Be perfect as your Heavenly Father is perfect," and I closed the book. I knew I could not live up to that standard, so my search for God began and ended there. Many Christians simply excuse these words of Jesus or talk around this demand of perfection. Is this really what God expects? What is a "real," born-again Christian supposed to look like?

The letter of First John was specifically written so that the readers would know if they could claim eternal life (1 John 5:13). Within that letter, John gives us very clear indicators. He says that someone born of God will not continue to practice sin, because Christ's seed is in him and he is born of God. He said that children of the devil and God are obviously distinguishable based on their ongoing sin or righteousness (1 John 3:4-10). He said that anyone who says they know Jesus and does not obey His teachings is a liar, and that those who know Him will walk as He walked (1 John 2:3-6). John likewise says that those who love the world or anything in the world do not love the Father (1 John 2:15-17). These teachings likely came from the words of Jesus Himself, who said that those who love Him obey His commands (John 4:15). The verdict is in: many who claim that they are born again, know Jesus, and love both the Father and the Son, fail to live up to the clear standards set forth for salvation in the inspired and authoritative Word of God.

Holiness and obedience are hallmarks of an authentic Christian. However, our heart motivation behind what we do is of equal priority. Paul said if we have all gifts, all signs and wonders, and sacrifice everything, but lack love, our works are nothing and profit nothing. There is no greater act of love than leading someone to freedom from darkness and bringing them into the light of eternal salvation. Freeing people from sicknesses or unclean spirits is an amazing act of love as well. We are commanded to do to others what we want them to do for us; if we have experienced freedom through Christ, we should want nothing more than to share it with others. However, we must be sure that we pursue these aims not out of selfish motivations or mere duty but rather, out of obedience and commitment to our Lord and love and mercy for our fellow man.

The sincerity and authenticity of our service for the Lord come from the Spirit and from our love for Jesus. We stay strong in fight by remaining in Christ and abiding in His word, but we cannot accomplish this in the flesh by acts of the will. God works it in us by His Spirit, always leading us deeper into His truth and drawing us closer to Him. God delivered the Israelites in a series of miraculous events that were designed to instill fear in the hearts of the Egyptians and compel them to release God's people from bondage. However, even afterward He did not leave His people to themselves. He continued to guide them, show His miracles, and reveal His great love for them as they journeyed to the Promised Land. In the same way, God is always at work in our lives and we should be alert for His movement and allow His presence to continually encourage us and strengthen us to press on in step with Him.

When we personally encounter God, with raw demonstrations of His power, we are slower to slink back into doubt and disillusionment. We need only remind ourselves of what we have seen Him do in our lives and in the lives of those around us. Doubt is a powerful tool of the enemy, but once it is overcome, we can find our walk dramatically changed—as did a brother of mine during my short trip to America.

Sure, he had heard all the reports. But *really*? Healings, demons, tongues...it all sounded just a bit crazy. My stateside brother knew that I wasn't making up these reports, but after watching some YouTube videos detailing how such healings are simply psychological tricks using hypnotism, he was extremely skeptical, even adversarial to the idea of "faith healing." As we fellowshipped and traveled together, I did not push the issue too hard. He was a sincere brother. He knew the voice of God. He just lacked firsthand experience with these things.

On our third day together visiting with brethren from our old home fellowship, opportunity presented itself. A boy had a terrible headache. I prayed, and he was immediately healed. Another brother had a longtime neck pain resulting from his occupation. I rebuked that condition and he was healed. Then some troubling spirits and strongholds were revealed in other brethren. We prayed for those, and each one experienced deliverance. We fellowshipped for hours and enjoyed each other's company before parting for the day.

The next day I received a phone call from the man with the hurting neck. He thanked me profusely because he had experienced no relief from this long-standing problem, and now it was indeed gone. I think he was somewhat surprised that even the next morning he would wake up without pain. I relayed the encouraging report to my doubting brother. He just took it all in.

Afterwards, we visited other brethren in another state. They also expressed their doubts about faith healing. I overheard my now-believing brother recounting the things he had seen just over the last few days. He reassured the others that they could simply trust and believe. He was transformed by what he had seen. But, as Jesus said, blessed are those who have not seen and yet believe. Indeed, we walk by faith and not by sight.

Of course our faith increases when we see God do amazing things around us and for us. However, even the Israelites had this experience, and we know that precious few of their number actually entered the Promised Land in the end. That is why this walk in the Spirit is of such great importance. We must be vigilant to continually maintain our fellowship with the Father: listening through fasting and prayer, obeying by His grace, serving others in love with the gifts He gives, and continually giving thanks for His personal work in our lives as we see Him move.

When we do not see God's hand at work in our lives, it is easy to cling to intellectual belief, as many of us Westerners tend to do when we come to faith through *information* rather than *transformation*. Our walk becomes more duty than desire, and we may fail to pursue holiness. The same was true for one of my Kenyan brothers, as the following story illustrates.

The car pulled right out into his motorbike and sent him flying over the handlebars into a roadside culvert. In that instant, the flipping motorcycle barreled right towards him at some 50 kilometers per hour. He was staring at imminent death. Suddenly, he felt something physically grab him and pull him out of the way of the oncoming motorcycle. It missed him. But how?

He was alive. Bruised up a bit, but miraculously alive. The owner of the car pulled over and they settled affairs street-side. Fault was assigned and a fair amount changed hands as compensation for damages. The car pulled away, yet brother Craig still pondered the event. Who had pulled him to safety? There was no one there! God had obviously sent an angel to save his life. He was in awe, and immediately called one of the brothers to share the testimony and praise God.

I had led this brother to repentance and faith through "wise and persuasive words." He was a sincere brother, but he struggled with personal issues that I knew to be strongholds. Finally, during a *kesha*, some of those strongholds were addressed in prayer and an unclean spirit renounced. It was just after this that he was miraculously rescued from death. He felt that God was confirming the newness of

Christianity Unleashed

life he had recently experienced in the Spirit, and his walk has begun to change with the revelation of such a personal God.

Perhaps you have become convinced of the kingdom message and responded with surrender and repentance. Maybe you have been baptized and walk in obedience to the Word the best you can. This was me, and many of my Kenyan brethren, before I re-encountered the Holy Spirit. I read the book of Acts with a sense of awe and longing, wondering why this was not my experience. In fact, why did it not seem to be the experience of anyone around me? Why were our churches full of outreaches and programs, yet so obviously lacking in the awe and excitement of daily seeing the signs, wonders, miracles, and amazing conversions recorded in the Scriptures? Mine had become a dry, boring, and sterile faith.

With this faith, I brought numerous people to an intellectual assent of the kingdom of God and even a sincere desire to follow Him. But I failed to see truly changed lives—lives marked by the total commitment to righteousness and the sense of adventure that I saw in the book of Acts. As I sought answers, Paul's statement resonated with me—that he delivered a faith not with wise and persuasive words, but a demonstration of the Spirit and of power (1 Corinthians 2:4). The teachings were validated by signs and wonders, various miracles, and gifts of the Holy Spirit (Hebrews 2:4). He also warned the Galatians to not let anyone bewitch them with theology, but to remember that the real gospel delivered to them was accompanied with the Holy Spirit and miracles (Galatians 3:1-5). Paul said the kingdom of God does not consist in words, but in power (1 Corinthians 4:20).

Likewise, James admonished the saints that human wisdom is simply worldly, carnal, and demonic (James 3:15). The author of Hebrews warned that those who tasted the Holy Spirit and powers of the age to come should not backslide to their destruction (Hebrews 6:4-6). Just as I did, I challenge you to read the book of Acts. See the awe and excitement, the sense of purpose and adventure of the first church; also note how they regularly met together to share meals, rejoice together, and spend time in prayer—all through the fellowship of the Spirit. Now, compare that to your Christian experience.

Look at Paul's conversion as an example of someone being *unleashed* from slavery and subsequently *unleashed* as a soldier for the kingdom. He persecuted the saints to imprisonment and death because of his religious strongholds. He was serving as a slave of Satan, but was deceived into thinking he was actually serving God. His transformation was initiated by a miraculous encounter with God, an event that would define the rest of his life, and of which we read repeatedly in the book of Acts.

He immediately fasted and was healed, baptized, and filled with the Holy Spirit upon his repentance. Paul was saved! So did he just start attending church weekly? No! Seeing what the power of God had done in his life, he went from *slave* to *soldier* instantly. He immediately surrendered everything he held dear in complete commitment to the Lord's service. He began proclaiming the kingdom of God, healing the sick, and expelling demons. He regularly heard from God through supernatural means. He would pray unceasingly and suffer severe persecution and loss as a soldier for Christ. He did not just teach with words, but demonstrated the power of the Holy Spirit. He was the ultimate example of the transformative power of God. But that is Paul—you know, the apostle. He is a super person. That certainly does not apply to you and me, right?

Knowing that we all, to some degree, accept the lie of mediocrity that Satan feeds us, I set out to write my testimony as an encouragement. Not because I am a super person, but because I am *not*. I am just Marc, a normal Christian serving an amazing God. But, like Paul, I needed an encounter with the power of God to experience the reality of the Holy Spirit. The transformation that has occurred in my life can happen to you, too. The things God is doing through me, He can easily do through you. I did not set out to write a theological work, but rather a practical, contemporary testimony so that you can trust that the things written in the Bible are for *you*, today. You just need to be *unleashed*—unleashed from what binds you and mobilized to action.

Have you had an undeniable, personal encounter with God that you can always come back to when doubt and disillusionment manifest? How do you know that the God you follow is real, and that His Word is true? Step out in faith and *believe, desire,* and *receive* all that He has for you. Unleash the potential within yourself. Unlock the authority God has given you in Jesus' name. Get off your seat and get engaged in the battle. The harvest is ready, but the laborers are few. Leave the sideline and enter the fight!

End Notes

---

i Barna Group, Inc. (September 15, 2016). The State of the Church 2016. Retrieved from http://www.barna.com/research/state-church-2016.

ii Barna Group, Inc. (April 6, 2016). The Priorities, Challenges, and Trends in Youth Ministry. Retrieved from http://www.barna.com/research/the-priorities-challenges-and-trends-in-youth-ministry

iii [When, therefore, the number of men had begun to increase, to whom from the beginning He had given power over the earth, God in His forethought sent angels for the protection and improvement of the human race, lest the devil should by his subtilty either corrupt or destroy men, as he had done at first;] and inasmuch as He had given these [the angels] a free will, He enjoined them above all things not to defile themselves with contamination from the earth, and thus lose the dignity of their heavenly nature. He plainly prohibited them from doing that which He knew that they would do, that they might entertain no hope of pardon. Therefore, while they abode among men, that most deceitful ruler of the earth, by his very association, gradually enticed them to vices, and polluted them by intercourse with women. Then, not being admitted into heaven on account of the sins into which they had plunged themselves, they fell to the earth. Thus from angels the devil makes them to become his satellites and attendants. But they who were born from these, because they were neither angels nor men, but bearing a kind of mixed nature, were not admitted into hell [Hades], as their fathers were not into heaven. Thus there came to be two kinds of demons; one of heaven, the other of the earth. The latter are the wicked spirits, the authors of all the evils which are done, and the same devil is their prince...And these, since spirits are without substance and not to be grasped, insinuate themselves into the bodies of men; and secretly working in their inward parts, they corrupt the health, hasten diseases, terrify their souls with dreams, harass their minds with frenzies. (Lactantius ANF v. 7, 64. c. 304-313 AD)

iv I would say, moreover, that, agreeably to the promise of Jesus, His disciples performed even greater works than these miracles of Jesus, which were perceptible only to the senses. For the eyes of those who are blind in soul are ever opened; and the ears of those who are deaf to virtuous words, listen readily to the doctrine of God, and of the blessed life with Him; and many, too, who were lame in the feet of the "inner man," as Scripture calls it, having now been healed by the word, do not simply leap, but leap as the hart, which is an animal hostile to serpents, and stronger than all the poison of vipers. And these lame who have been healed, receive from Jesus power to trample, with those feet in which they were formerly lame, upon the serpents and scorpions of wickedness, and generally upon all the power of the enemy;

and though they tread upon it, they sustain no injury, for they also have become stronger than the poison of all evil and of demons. (Origen ANF v. 4, 450. c. 248 AD)

v Those who are truly His disciples, receiving grace from Him, perform [miraculous works] in His name, in order to promote the welfare of others, according to the gift that each one has received from Him. Some truly and certainly cast out devils. The result is that those who have been cleansed from evil spirits frequently both believe and join themselves to the church. Others have foreknowledge of things to come. They see visions, and they utter prophetic expressions. Still others heal the sick by laying their hands upon them, and the sick are made whole. What is more, as I have said, even the dead have been raised up and remained among us for many years. What more can I say? It is not possible to name the number of the gifts which the church throughout the whole world has received from God, in the name of Jesus Christ, who was crucified under Pontius Pilate and which she exerts day by day for the benefit of the Gentiles, neither practicing deception upon any, nor taking any reward from them. For, just as she has received without charge from God, so does she minister without charge. Nor does she perform anything by means of angelic invocations, incantations, or any other wicked curious art. Calling upon the name of our Lord Jesus Christ, she has worked miracles for the benefit of mankind, and not to lead them into error. The name of our Lord Jesus Christ even now confers benefits. It cures thoroughly and effectively all who anywhere believe on Him. (Irenaeus ANF v. 1, 409. c. 180 AD)

vi JESUS CHRIST, our God and Saviour, delivered to us the great mystery of godliness, and called both Jews and Gentiles to the acknowledgment of the one and only true God His Father, as Himself somewhere says, when He was giving thanks for the salvation of those that had believed, "I have manifested Thy name to men, I have finished the work Thou gavest me;" and said concerning us to His Father, "Holy Father, although the world has not known Thee, yet have I known Thee; and these have known Thee." With good reason did He say to all of us together, when we were perfected concerning those gifts which were given from Him by the Spirit: "Now these signs shall follow them that have believed in my name: they shall cast out devils; they shall speak with new tongues; they shall take up serpents; and if they drink any deadly thing, it shall by no means hurt them: they shall lay their hands on the sick, and they shall recover." These gifts were first bestowed on us the apostles when we were about to preach the gospel to every creature, and afterwards were of necessity afforded to those who had by our means believed; not for the advantage of those who perform them, but for the conviction of the unbelievers, that those whom the word did not persuade, the power of signs might put to shame: for signs are not for us who believe, but for the unbelievers, both for the Jews and Gentiles. For neither is it any profit to us to cast out demons, but to those who are so cleansed by the power of the Lord; as the Lord Himself somewhere instructs us, and shows, saying: "Rejoice ye, not because the spirits are subject unto you; but rejoice, because your names are written in heaven." Since the former is done by His power, but this by our good disposition and diligence, yet (it is manifest) by His assistance. It is not therefore necessary that every one of the faithful should cast out demons, or raise the dead, or speak with tongues; but such a one only who is vouchsafed this gift, for some cause which may be advantage to the salvation of the unbelievers, who are often put to shame, not with the demonstration of the world, but by the power of the signs; that is, such as are worthy of salvation: for all the ungodly are not affected by wonders; and hereof God Himself is a witness, as when He says in the law: "With other tongues will I speak to this people, and with other lips, and yet will they by no means believe." (Apostolic Constitutions ANF v. 7, 479. compiled c. 390 AD)

vii and the apostle most assuredly foretold that there were to be "spiritual gifts" in the church. (Tertullian ANF v. 3, 188. c. 210 AD)

viii Archelaus said: Those sayings which are put forth by the blessed Paul were not uttered without the direction of God, and therefore it is certain that what he has declared to us is that we are to look for our Lord Jesus Christ as the perfect one, who is the only one that knows the Father, with the sole exception of him to whom He has chosen also to reveal Him, as I am able to demonstrate from His own words. But let it be observed, that it is said that when that which is perfect is come, then that which is in part shall be done away...For in that first Epistle to the Corinthians, Paul speaks in the following terms of the perfection that is to come: "Whether there be prophecies, they shall fail; whether there be tongues, they shall cease; whether there be knowledge, it shall be destroyed: for we know in part, and we prophesy in part; but when that which is perfect is come, then that which is in part shall be done away." Observe now what virtue that which is perfect possesses in itself, and of what order that perfection is...But not thus inconsiderable, not thus obscure and ignoble, will be the manner of the advent of Him who is the truly perfect one, that is to say, our Lord Jesus Christ. Nay, but as a king, when he draws near to his city, does first of all send on before him his life-guardsmen, his ensigns and standards and banners, his generals and chiefs and prefects, and then forthwith all objects are roused and excited in different fashions, while some become inspired with terror and others with exultation at the prospect of the king's advent; so also my Lord Jesus Christ, who is the truly perfect one, at His coming will first send on before Him His glory, and the consecrated heralds of an unstained and untainted kingdom: and then the universal creation will be moved and perturbed, uttering prayers and supplications, until He delivers it from its bondage. And it must needs be that the race of man shall then be in fear and in vehement agitation on account of the many offences it has committed. Then the righteous alone will rejoice, as they look for the things which have been promised them; and the subsistence of the affairs of this world will no longer be maintained, but all things shall be destroyed: and whether they be prophecies or the books of prophets, they shall fail; whether they be the tongues of the whole race, they shall cease; for men will no longer need to feel anxiety or to think solicitously about those things which are necessary for life; whether it be knowledge, by what teachers soever it be possessed, it shall also be destroyed: for none of all these things will be able to endure the advent of that mighty King. For just as a little spark, if taken and put up against the splendour of the sun, at once perishes from the view, so the whole creation, all prophecy, all knowledge, all tongues, as we have said above, shall be destroyed. (Disputation of Archelaus and Manes ANF v. 6, 211. c. 320 AD)

ix For they [the Jews] have no longer prophets nor miracles, traces of which to a considerable extent are still found among Christians, and some of them more remarkable than any that existed among the Jews; and these we ourselves have witnessed, if our testimony may be received. (Origen ANF v. 4, 433. c. 248)

x Now compare the Spirit's specific graces, as they are described by the apostle, and promised by the prophet Isaiah. "To one is given," says he, "by the Spirit the word of wisdom;" this we see at once is what Isaiah declared to be "the spirit of wisdom." "To another, the word of knowledge;" this will be "the (prophet's) spirit of understanding and counsel." "To another, faith by the same Spirit;" this will be "the spirit of religion and the fear of the Lord." "To another, the gifts of healing, and to another the working of miracles;" this will be "the spirit of might." "To another prophecy, to another discerning of spirits, to another divers kinds of tongues, to another the interpretation of tongues;" this will be "the spirit of knowledge." See how the apostle agrees with the prophet both in making the distribution of the one Spirit, and in interpreting His special graces. ... (Tertullian ANF v. 3, 446. C. 207 AD)

xi the same Spirit, having in themselves the gifts which this same Spirit distributes, and appropriates to the Church, the spouse of Christ, as her ornaments. This is He who places prophets in the Church, instructs teachers, directs tongues, gives powers and healings, does wonderful works, offers discrimination of spirits, affords powers of government, suggests counsels, and orders and arranges whatever other gifts there are of charismata; and thus make the Lord's Church everywhere, and in all, perfected and completed. This is He who, after the manner of a dove, when our Lord was baptized, came and abode upon Him, dwelling in Christ full and entire, and not maimed in any measure or portion; but with His whole overflow copiously distributed and sent forth, so that from Him others might receive some enjoyment of His graces: the source of the entire Holy Spirit remaining in Christ, so that from Him might be drawn streams of gifts and works, while the Holy Spirit dwelt affluently in Christ. (Novatian ANF v. 5, 640. c. 235 AD)

xii It is true that believers likewise "have the Spirit of God;" but not all believers are apostles. When then, he who had called himself a "believer," added thereafter that he "had the Spirit of God," which no one would doubt even in the case of an (ordinary) believer; his reason for saying so was, that he might reassert for himself apostolic dignity. For apostles have the Holy Spirit properly, who have Him fully, in the operations of prophecy, and the efficacy of (healing) virtues, and the evidences of tongues; not partially, as all others have. Tertullian ANF v. 4, 53, c. 212 AD)

xiii For we call Him Helper and Redeemer, the power of whose name even the demons do fear; and at this day, when they are exorcised in the name of Jesus Christ..., they are overcome. And thus it is manifest to all, that His Father has given Him so great power, by virtue of which demons are subdued to His name. (Justin Martyr ANF v. 1, 209. c. 160 AD)

xiv When he mentions the fact that "it is written in the law," how that the Creator would speak with other tongues and other lips, whilst confirming indeed the gift of tongues by such a mention, he yet cannot be thought to have affirmed that the gift was that of another god by his reference to the Creator's prediction. (Tertullian v. 3, 446. c. 207 AD)

xv And there are still preserved among Christians traces of that Holy Spirit which appeared in the form of a dove. They expel evil spirits, and perform many cures, and foresee certain events, according to the will of the Logos. (Origen ANF v. 4, 415. c. 248)

xvi [We] can clearly show a countless multitude of Greeks and Barbarians who acknowledge the existence of Jesus. And some give evidence of their having received through this faith a marvellous power by the cures which they perform, revoking no other name over those who need their help than that of the God of all things, and of Jesus, along with a mention of His history. For by these means we too have seen many persons freed from grievous calamities, and from distractions of mind, and madness, and countless other ills, which could be cured neither by men nor devils. (Origen ANF v. 4, 473. c. 248 AD)

xvii Now was absolutely fulfilled that promise of the Spirit which was given by the word of Joel: "In the last days will I pour out of my Spirit upon all flesh, and their sons and their daughters shall prophesy; and upon my servants and upon my handmaids will I pour out of my Spirit." Since, then, the Creator promised the gift of His Spirit in the latter days; and since Christ has in these last days appeared as the dispenser of spiritual gifts (as the apostle says, "When the fulness of the time was come, God sent forth His Son;" and again, "This I say, brethren, that the time is short"), it evidently follows in connection with this prediction of the last days, that this gift of the Spirit belongs to Him who is the Christ of the predicter. (Tertullian ANF v. 3, 446. c. 207 AD) xviii But to the Father of all, who is unbegotten there is no name given. For by whatever name He be called, He has as His elder the person who gives Him the name. But these words Father, and God, and Creator, and Lord, and Master, are not names, but appellations derived from His good deeds and functions. And His Son, who alone is properly called Son, the Word who also was with Him and was begotten before the works, when at first He created and arranged all things by Him, is called Christ, in reference to His being anointed and God's ordering all things through Him; this name itself also containing an unknown significance; as also the appellation "God" is not a name, but an opinion implanted in the nature of men of a thing that can hardly be explained. But "Jesus," His name as man and Saviour, has also significance. For He was made man also, as we before said, having been conceived according to the will of God the Father, for the sake of believing men, and for the destruction of the demons. And now you can learn this from what is under your own observation. For numberless demoniacs throughout the whole world, and in your city, many of our Christian men exorcising them in the name of Jesus Christ, who was crucified under Pontius Pilate, have healed and do heal, rendering helpless and driving the possessing devils out of the men, though they could not be cured by all the other exorcists, and those who used incantations and drugs. (Justin Martyr ANF v. 1, 190. c. 160 AD)

xix Moreover, by His own power He not only performed those miraculous deeds which have been detailed by us in summary, and not as the importance of the matter demanded; but, what was more sublime, He has permitted many others to attempt them, and to perform them by the use of His name. For when He foresaw that you were to be the detractors of His deeds and of His divine work, in order that no lurking suspicion might remain of His having lavished these gifts and bounties by magic arts, from the immense multitude of people, which with admiring wonder strove to gain His favour, He chose fishermen, artisans, rustics, and unskilled persons of a similar kind, that they being sent through various nations should perform all those miracles without any deceit and without any material aids. (Arnobius ANF v. 6, 427. c. 305 AD)

xx He said, 'I give unto you power to tread on serpents, and on scorpions, and on [centipedes], and on all the might of the enemy.' And now we, who believe on our Lord Jesus..., when we exorcise all demons and evil spirits, have them subjected to us. (Justin Martyr ANF v. 1, 236. c. 160 AD)

xxi It is manifest, therefore, that the ungodly, although they prophesy, do not by their prophesying cover their own impiety; nor will those who cast out demons be sanctified by the demons being made subject to them: for they...destroy those who give heed to them. (Apostolic Constitutions ANF v. 7, 481. compiled c. 390 AD) xxii Is it not, then, a miserable inference, to conclude from the same works that the one is God and the other sorcerers? Why ought the others, because of these acts, to be accounted wicked rather than this man, seeing they have him as their witness against himself? For he has himself acknowledged that these are not the works of a divine nature, but the inventions of certain deceivers, and of thoroughly wicked men." Observe, now, whether Celsus is not clearly convicted of slandering the gospel by such statements, since what Jesus says regarding those who are to work signs and wonders is different from what this Jew of Celsus alleges it to be. For if Jesus had simply told His disciples to be on their guard against those who professed to work miracles, without declaring what they would give themselves out to be, then perhaps there would have been some ground for his suspicion. But since those against whom Jesus would have us to be on our guard give themselves out as the Christ—which is not a claim put forth by sorcerers—and since He says that even some who lead wicked lives will perform miracles in the name of Jesus, and expel demons out of men, sorcery in the case of these individuals, or any suspicion of such, is rather, if we may so speak, altogether banished, and the divinity of Christ established, as well as the divine mission of His disciples; seeing that it is possible that one who makes use of His name, and who is wrought upon by some power, in some way unknown, to make the pretence that he is the Christ, should seem to perform miracles like those of Jesus, while others through His name should do works resembling those of His genuine disciples. (Origen ANF v. 4, 450. c. 248 AD)

xxiii ...demons which many Christians cast out of persons possessed with them. And this, we may observe, they do without the use of any curious arts of magic, or incantations, but merely by prayer and simple adjurations which the plainest person can use. Because for the most part it is unlettered persons who perform this work; thus making manifest the grace which is in the word of Christ, and the despicable weakness of demons, which, in order to be overcome and driven out of the bodies and souls of men, do not require the power and wisdom of those who are mighty in argument, and most learned in matters of faith. (Origen ANF v. 4, 612. c. 248 AD)

xxiv An exorcist is not ordained. For it is a trial of voluntary goodness, and of the grace of God through Christ by the inspiration of the Holy Spirit. (Apostolic Constitutions v. 7, 493. compiled c. 390 AD)

xxv God, when He had made the whole world, and subjected things earthly to man, and arranged the heavenly elements for the increase of fruits and rotation of the seasons, and appointed this divine law—for these things also He evidently made for man—committed the care of men and of all things under heaven to angels whom He appointed over them. But the angels transgressed this appointment, and were captivated by love of women, and begat children who are those that are called demons; and besides, they afterwards subdued the human race to themselves, partly by magical writings, and partly by fears and the punishments they occasioned, and partly by teaching them to offer sacrifices, and incense, and libations, of which things they stood in need after they were enslaved by lustful passions; and among men they sowed murders, wars, adulteries, intemperate deeds, and all wickedness. (Justin Martyr v 1. 190. c. 160 AD)

xxvi When Almighty God, to beautify the nature of the world, willed that that earth should be visited by angels, when they were sent down they despised His laws. Such was the beauty of women, that it turned them aside; so that, being contaminated, they could not return to heaven. Rebels from God, they uttered words against Him. Then the Highest uttered His judgment against them; and from their seed giants are said to have been born...But the Almighty, because they were of an evil seed, did not approve that, when dead, they should be brought back from death. Whence wandering they now subvert many bodies, and it is such as these especially that ye this day worship and pray to as gods. (Commodianus ANF v. 4, 203. c. 240 AD)

xxvii Now, of wicked spirits there is a twofold mode of operation: i.e., when they either take complete and entire possession of the mind, so as to allow their captives the power neither of understanding nor feeling; as, for instance, is the case with those commonly called possessed, whom we see to be deprived of reason, and insane (such as those were who are related in the gospel to have been cured by the Saviour); or when by their wicked suggestions they deprave a sentient and intelligent soul with thoughts of various kinds, persuading it to evil. (Origen ANF v. 4, 336. c. 225 AD)

xxviii We do not, then, deny that there are many demons upon earth, but we maintain that they exist and exercise power among the wicked, as a punishment of their wickedness. But they have no power over those who "have put on the whole armour of God," who have received strength to "withstand the wiles of the devil," and who are ever engaged in contests with them, knowing that "we wrestle not against flesh and blood, but against principalities, against powers, against the rulers of the darkness of this world, against spiritual wickedness in high places." (Origen ANF v. 4, 653. c. 248 AD)

xxix the Architect of the universe Himself, in keeping with the marvellously persuasive power of His words, commended Him [Jesus] as worthy of honour, not only to those men who were well disposed, but to demons also, and other unseen powers, which even at the present time show that they either fear the name of Jesus as that of a being of superior power, or reverentially accept Him as their legal ruler. For if the commendation had not been given Him by God, the demons would not have withdrawn from those whom they had assailed, in obedience to the mere mention of His name. (Origen ANF v. 4, 279. c. 248, AD) xxx The practice of insufflation and exsufflation were common in religious ritual, particularly baptisms and exorcisms: Isufflation. (n.d.). In Wikipedia. Retrieved August 10, 2017.

xxxi And the name of Jesus can still remove distractions from the minds of men, and expel demons, and also take away diseases; and produce a marvellous meekness of spirit and complete change of character, and a humanity, and goodness, and gentleness in those individuals who do not feign themselves to be Christians for the sake of subsistence or the supply of any mortal wants, but who have honestly accepted the doctrine concerning God and Christ, and the judgment to come. (Origen ANF v. 4, 427. c. 248 AD)

xxxii Wherefore let none of you exalt himself against his brother, though he be a prophet, or though he be a worker of miracles: for if it happens that there be no longer an unbeliever, all the power of signs will thenceforwards be superfluous. (Apostolic Constitutions ANF v. 7, 480. compiled c. 390 AD)

xxxiii For the prophetical gifts remain with us, even to the present time. And hence you ought to understand that [the gifts] formerly among your nation [the Jews] have been transferred to us. Justin Martyr ANF v. 1, 240 (c. 160 AD)

xxxiv Wretched men indeed! who wish to be pseudo-prophets, forsooth, but who set aside the gift of prophecy from the Church...hold themselves aloof from the communion of the brethren. We must conclude, moreover, that these men (the Montanists) can not admit the Apostle Paul either. For, in his Epistle to the Corinthians, he speaks expressly of prophetical gifts, and recognises men and women prophesying in the Church. (Irenaeus ANF v. 1, 429. c. 180 AD)

In precisely the same manner, when enjoining on women silence in the church, that they speak not for the mere sake of learning (although that even they have the right of prophesying, he has already shown when he covers the woman that prophesies with a veil), he goes to the law for his sanction that woman should be under obedience. (Tertullian ANF v. 3, 446. c. 207 AD)

xxxv Wherefore if among you also there be a man or a woman, and such a one obtains any gift, let him be humble, that God may be pleased with him. (Apostolic Constitutions ANF v. 7, 481. compiled c. 390 AD)

xxxvi Moreover, the order of reason, and the authority of the faith in the disposition of the words and in the Scriptures of the Lord, admonish us after these things to believe also on the Holy Spirit, once promised to the Church, and in the appointed occasions of times given. For He was promised by Joel the prophet, but given by Christ. "In the last days," says the prophet, "I will pour out of my Spirit upon my servants and my handmaids." And the Lord said, "Receive ye the Holy Ghost: whose sins ye remit, they shall be remitted; and whose ye retain, they shall be retained." But this Holy Spirit the Lord Christ calls at one time "the Paraclete," at another pronounces to be the "Spirit of truth." And He is not new in the gospel, nor yet even newly given; for it was He Himself who accused the people in the prophets, and in the apostles gave them the appeal to the Gentiles. For the former deserved to be accused, because they had contemned the law; and they of the Gentiles who believe deserve to be aided by the defence of the Spirit, because they earnestly desire to attain to the gospel law. Assuredly in the Spirit there are different kinds of offices, because in the times there is a different order of occasions; and yet, on this account, He who discharges these offices is not different, nor is He another in so acting, but He is one and the same, distributing His offices according to the times, and the occasions and impulses of things. Moreover, the Apostle Paul says, "Having the same Spirit; as it is written, I believed, and therefore have I spoken; we also believe, and therefore speak." He is therefore one and the same Spirit who was in the prophets and apostles, except that in the former He was occasional, in the latter always. But in the former not as being always in them, in the latter as abiding always in them; and in the former distributed with reserve, in the latter all poured out; in the former given sparingly, in the latter liberally bestowed; not yet manifested before the Lord's resurrection, but conferred after the resurrection. For, said He, "I will pray the Father, and He will give you another Advocate, that He may be with you for ever, even the Spirit of truth." And, "When He, the Advocate, shall come, whom I shall send unto you from my Father, the Spirit of truth who proceedeth from my Father." And, "If I go not away, that Advocate shall not come to you; but if I go away, I will send Him to you." And, "When the Spirit of truth shall come, He will direct you into all the truth." And because the Lord was about to depart to the heavens, He gave the Paraclete out of necessity to the disciples; so as not to leave them in any degree orphans, which was little desirable, and forsake them without an advocate and some kind of protector. For this is He who strengthened their hearts and minds, who marked out the gospel sacraments, who was in them the enlightener of divine things; and they being strengthened, feared, for the sake of the Lord's name, neither dungeons nor chains, nay, even trod under foot the very powers of the world and its tortures, since they were henceforth armed and strengthened by the same Spirit, having in themselves the gifts which this same Spirit distributes, and appropriates to the Church, the spouse of Christ, as her ornaments. This is He who places prophets in the Church, instructs teachers, directs tongues, gives powers and healings, does wonderful works, offers discrimination of spirits, affords powers of government, suggests counsels, and orders and arranges whatever other gifts there are of charismata; and thus make the Lord's Church everywhere, and in all, perfected and completed. This is He who, after the manner of a dove, when our Lord was baptized, came and abode upon Him, dwelling in Christ full and entire, and not maimed in any measure or portion; but with His whole overflow copiously distributed and sent forth, so that from Him others might receive some enjoyment of His graces: the source of the entire Holy Spirit remaining in Christ, so that from Him might be drawn streams of gifts and works, while the Holy Spirit dwelt affluently in Christ. For truly Isaiah, prophesying this, said: "And the Spirit of wisdom and understanding shall rest upon Him, the Spirit of counsel and might, the Spirit of knowledge and piety; and the Spirit of the fear of the Lord shall fill Him." This self-same thing also he said in the person of the Lord Himself, in another place, "The Spirit of the Lord is upon me; because He has anointed me, He has sent me to preach the gospel to the poor." Similarly David: "Wherefore God, even Thy God, hath anointed Thee with the oil of gladness above thy fellows." Of Him the Apostle Paul says: "For he who hath not the Spirit of Christ is none of His." "And where the Spirit of the Lord is, there is liberty." He it is who effects with water the second birth as a certain seed of divine generation, and a consecration of a heavenly nativity, the pledge of a promised inheritance, and as it were a kind of handwriting of eternal salvation; who can make us God's temple, and fit us for His house; who solicits the divine hearing for us with groanings that cannot be uttered; filling the offices of advocacy, and manifesting the duties of our defence,—an inhabitant given for our bodies and an effector of their holiness. Who, working in us for eternity, can also produce our bodies at the resurrection of immortality, accustoming them to be associated in Himself with heavenly power, and to be allied with the divine eternity of the Holy Spirit. For our bodies are both trained in Him and by Him to advance to immortality, by learning to govern themselves with moderation according to His decrees. For this is He who "desireth against the flesh," because "the flesh resisteth against the Spirit." This is He who restrains insatiable desires, controls immoderate lusts, quenches unlawful fires, conquers reckless impulses, repels drunkenness, checks avarice, drives away luxurious revellings, links love, binds together affections, keeps down sects, orders the rule of truth, overcomes heretics, turns out the wicked, guards the gospel. Of this says the same apostle: "We have not received the spirit of the world, but the Spirit which is of God." Concerning Him he exultingly says: "And I think also that I have the Spirit of God." Of Him he says: "The Spirit of the prophets is subject to the prophets." Of Him also he tells: "Now the Spirit speaketh plainly, that in the last times some shall depart from the faith, giving heed to seducing spirits, doctrines of demons, who speak lies in hypocrisy, having their conscience cauterized." Established in this Spirit, "none ever calleth Jesus anathema;" no one has ever denied Christ to be the Son of God, or has rejected God the Creator; no one utters any words of his own contrary to the Scriptures; no one ordains other and sacrilegious decrees; no one draws up different laws. Whosoever shall blaspheme against Him, "hath not forgiveness, not only in this world, but also not in the world to come." This is He who in the apostles gives testimony to Christ; in the martyrs shows forth the constant faithfulness of their religion; in virgins restrains the admirable continency of their sealed chastity; in others, guards the laws of the Lord's doctrine incorrupt and uncontaminated; destroys heretics, corrects the perverse, condemns infidels, makes known pretenders; moreover, rebukes the wicked, keeps the Church uncorrupt and inviolate, in the sanctity of a perpetual virginity and truth. (Novatian ANF v. 5, 640-641. c. 235 AD)

Made in the USA
Monee, IL
25 February 2023